2

Practical
Sponsorship

Practical Sponsorship

Stuart Turner

**Kogan
Page**

First published in Great Britain
in 1987 by Kogan Page Limited,
120 Pentonville Road, London N1 9JN

British Library Cataloguing in Publication Data

Turner, Stuart
    Practical sponsorship.
    1. Advertising — Great Britain 2. Performing
    arts sponsorship — Great Britain 3. Sports
    — Sponsorship — Great Britain
    I. Title
    658.8'2   HF5827
    ISBN 1–85091–245–9

Printed and bound in Great Britain
by Billings & Sons Limited, Worcester.

Contents

Appendices

Introduction

In recent years sponsorship has become a growth industry, with almost anything sponsored from music festivals to upmarket activities like mud-wrestling. The result has been extensive media coverage but newcomers to sponsorship should not be awed by the hype nor by any apparent glamour or mystique. No special training or qualifications are needed to get involved in sponsorship – just commonsense and a little flair – and there is no reason why a newcomer's sponsorship should not be as successful as anyone else's. But it is important to remain in touch with reality. Businessmen should not lose their normal commercial acumen at the thrill of touching the hem of a sports star's shirt, and sportsmen and those in the arts should not assume that sponsorship is an instant panacea for their financial ills – it is a buyer's market and finding support is not easy.

The first part of this book looks at things from the sponsor's viewpoint, the second considers how people can find, and equally important, retain sponsorship. I suggest that both groups should read the whole book because having an awareness of the other person's needs will make both sponsoring and finding sponsorship that much easier.

Finally, let me stress that the use of male pronouns and examples throughout is purely for euphony – women can be just as active and successful in sponsorship as men.

Stuart Turner

Part 1

How to Sponsor

Chapter 1 **Background**

If you are a bright-eyed executive and your quality circles are circulating smoothly and you have come to terms with your desktop terminal, you may feel that sponsorship is the latest business tool to help you in your search for excellence. Well, the last thing I want to do is dampen your enthusiasm, but sponsorship isn't all that new. In the arts, kings and other members of the upper crust have thrown crumbs to painters, poets and playwrights for centuries, while in sport my guess is that when David and Goliath had their all-comers contest, the little guy was probably sponsored by 'Slings and Arrows', an outrageous fortune-telling operation (franchised, of course). Over 100 years ago the *Blackburn Times* reported that a local iron foundry owner had 'sponsored a football team by a donation of £100'. Note the use of the word 'sponsored' and note too the amount involved – £100 was an enormous sum in those days and the foundry owner's generosity could well have started the phrase 'where there's muck there's brass'.

So sponsorship has a long history. But just what is it? Well, it straddles so many business disciplines that I am tempted to leave a blank space for you to write your own definition because sponsorship is almost what you care to make it, but try this:

X Sponsorship is the provision of support by a person or company for some independent activity (usually related to sport or the arts, although the field is widening) not directly linked to the person's or company's normal business, but support from which the sponsor hopes to benefit.

The support can be financial or material, while the activity sponsored should be independent of the sponsor, otherwise the action is purely sales promotion. Sponsorship is a business tool, not a cause, and should always be two-way, with a sponsor expecting to get something in return for support, say increased sales or an enhanced reputation. Happily, sponsorship will often be seen to be good citizenship, benefiting a community and/or improving the quality of life, and the goodwill from this may be enough reward for many companies but, whatever the circumstances, a sponsor should be expecting to get a clear benefit of some sort otherwise his support becomes charity or patronage (too many sponsorship links become these because they are so badly handled that sponsors get little in return for their money, but that's another story).

Incidentally, while we're considering definitions remember that an *endorsement* is usually just a paid-for recommendation, although many such arrangements stem naturally from sponsorship links or are built into them from the start.

Sponsorship is not advertising, although it will often come out of the same budget, nor is it necessarily a substitute for a hard-hitting advertising campaign. With an advertisement you control your message and how and where it appears; you have less control with sponsorship where the impact may depend on the number of spectators, media attitudes and so on. And you will certainly have less control if one of your sponsored stars puts his foot in it; a not infrequent occurrence.

Spending money on advertisements will usually be 'safer' than sponsoring because the results may be more predictable; as we shall see, it is not easy to measure scientifically the effects of sponsorship. For many years advertising agencies were leery of sponsorship, perhaps because they considered it a threat to their billings, although things are changing and brighter agencies are forming their own sponsorship companies or forging links with existing ones.

The lines between sponsorship and advertising can get decidedly blurred. If you put a poster on the back of a bus we can probably agree that that is advertising. But what if you decorate the whole bus in your house colours? Advertising or sponsorship? Many would say it was still advertising but if your support helps to maintain a local service or to take deprived children to the seaside then it really becomes sponsorship.

What about a logo or company name on a sportsman's shirt? Arguably that is straightforward advertising but because it is an unconventional medium, it is likely to be called, and seen as, sponsorship. The same applies to display banners at sporting events featuring company names. If you can buy them without having a formal link with the activity, then that is advertising. It becomes sponsorship if the banners come as part of a package which includes, say, hospitality facilities and the supply of trophies. You can see how confusing it can become.

The lines between sponsorship and sales promotion get

equally blurred. If a bicycle manufacturing company enters a team in the Tour de France it is likely to be called sponsorship, but strictly speaking it is sales promotion; remember the point in the definition about the sponsor being independent of the sponsored. It just illustrates that sponsorship is something of a hybrid activity which spreads over advertising, sales promotion and, not least, public relations. I say 'not least' because if you don't take this side seriously then any sponsorship is likely to be a disappointment.

Hybrid it may be but research indicates that a high percentage of marketing people regard sponsorship as a Good Thing. Admittedly some of it is done for rather casual reasons – either because of pressure from a customer or because a decision-maker in a company falls in love with an activity. You really need more considered reasons for spending money, which is why planning is emphasized so much throughout this book.

There are three main reasons why companies sponsor; to promote public awareness, to entertain customers and to build goodwill. Perm any of those and they should help to create for a sponsor a more favourable climate in which to trade. And businessmen are going to need such climatic control because as people become more mobile, traditional customer loyalties tend to break down. Couple this with the remarkable changes in the media world which, among other things, offer sponsors multi-national marketing opportunities and I am on safe ground in forecasting that sponsorship will grow for a while yet. Apart from increased mobility, consider other social changes too. People will have more leisure time through shorter working hours, early retirement or, unhappily, unemployment. More leisure will lead to a demand for better facilities for sports and the arts, but if central funding stays scarce (as it will), where will people look? That's right, that's opportunity you can hear knocking because they will turn to industry for sponsorship. The continued scramble for funds will mean that apart from a handful of prime events, sponsorship will remain strictly a buyer's market. The sports, arts and so on will need money but companies will always have alternatives to sponsorship.

My second forecast (and the joy of making them is that people rarely check back, which is why economists are held in such absurd awe) is that the major growth in sponsorship will come in community projects, conservation and the like. Increasingly society will expect companies to do more than blindly chase profits without any thought for the community around them.

To give you an idea of the present scale of the sponsorship world, it is believed that the money spent on it represents only around four per cent of the UK advertising spend on press and TV advertising, with three-quarters going on sport and the rest split roughly 50/50 between the arts and other activities like conservation. Four per cent may not sound much but bear in mind that relatively few companies are yet involved. The number is growing, to the extent that before too long sponsorship could become almost an essential part of a company's marketing mix, with those not sponsoring something seen as just a shade out of touch, even old-fashioned.

X Not everyone is wild about the growth of sponsorship and voices can occasionally be heard crying 'enough'. Some regard sponsorship as an intrusion into sport and, for example, many are against a sponsor's name being incorporated in that of a team. There are ethical and moral concerns too; some consider that sponsorship demeans sport – skiers' frantic scrambles to remove their skis to show their sponsors' names on TV look rather silly for instance (and isn't it a moment to cherish when one falls over in his haste?). Certainly there have been occasions when an influx of money has thrown a sport off balance; some sportsmen have ended up with so much money that they've been able to run cars they couldn't even spell. Things become particularly dangerous if sponsorship can make or break a sport or if a sponsor shifts his stance from 'it's nice to be involved' to 'let me have control'. Governing bodies of sport need to encourage sponsors and set their stalls out to attract them, yet at the same time they must keep a balance between the stars and the grass roots participants. In the arts, some fear that sponsorship may encourage a safe, middle-of-the-road approach which stifles innovation.

The political dangers for sponsors themselves are all too apparent. Major sponsored events attract high media attention and may be irresistible platforms for politicians with axes to grind. At one sponsored event I attended a protester even held up a banner to the cameras reading 'Free Wales', although the impact was rather diluted because someone had scribbled underneath 'From what? For what?'

Sponsorship certainly becomes 'political', or at least controversial, when tobacco companies are involved. It is perhaps significant that far more paper cascaded through my letterbox on this subject than on any other when I was writing this book. Research suggests that broadly 50 per cent of people are happy about tobacco sponsorship; older people, not surprisingly, tend to support it more than the young. However, the 'anti' lobby is highly effective (though the British Medical Association does tend to go over the top at times) and there are even rumblings from non-tobacco sponsors that the controversies which tend to arise when cigarette companies are involved – the somewhat uneasy business of taping over sponsors' names and so on – have a deleterious effect on sponsorship as a whole. Because of the intense public debate, the representatives of some activities have themselves announced that they will not accept tobacco sponsorship, while actors have refused to appear in plays receiving such support.

But we need not dwell on the subject. Only a handful of people are involved in making sponsorship decisions for tobacco companies and I am sure that they don't need any advice from me. However, I can't accept that sport or the arts would collapse without tobacco funding, because only around 15 per cent of sports sponsorship comes from tobacco and drink combined, while only 1 per cent of theatre funding comes from cigarettes. Some activities would suffer for a while but if a total ban on tobacco support meant that a few superstars ended with lighter wallets and their feet slightly closer to the ground, I'm not sure that the world would stop.

Following tobacco I suppose the 'anti' brigade will set off after alcohol (where will it all end?) and there are already adverse press comments whenever a drinks company sponsors a sporting activity.

But enough. Drink up and let us move on to look at the benefits sponsorship can offer.

Chapter 2 **What Sponsorship Offers**

As we have considered, sponsorship should be a two-way affair so, assuming you are thinking of becoming a sponsor, what can you expect to get in return for your money? Well, first, an intangible but important *extra dimension* to your business activities because sponsorship offers additional opportunities to public relations and advertising. Even if you simply put your name on a litter-bin, which is really just advertising, calling it sponsorship and signwriting the bin 'sponsored by Harrisons' will add overtones of community involvement and good citizenship. If you get more heavily involved and sponsor a significant sporting or artistic event, you will be able to create greater promotional opportunities than through more conventional marketing action. And in a cost-effective way too because you can undertake large scale sponsorship for the cost of a very mild national press or TV advertising campaign.

But be cautious about drawing too many direct comparisons between paid advertising and sponsorship. A TV shot of a sponsor's name on a banner will be spotted by all the sponsor's employees but may go unnoticed by everyone else if they are watching the actual heart of the action, such as an athlete at full stretch; the public are less likely to miss a television commercial and may therefore be more influenced by it. However, they may of course be irritated or offended by a commercial, which is where sponsorship scores because it can be more subtle and seen as less intrusive and annoying than advertising. Because the activity being sponsored 'says' something about a sponsor (conveying an impression of excitement, modernity or whatever) sponsorship can certainly be more effective for instance than corporate advertising, some of which does tend to be rather bland. And consider for a moment: if you read an advertisement for a product then someone personally recommends a different one, which has the most impact on you? The personal plug, I suspect. Press coverage of a sponsored activity will operate in a not dissimilar fashion compared to a paid-for advertisement, because as editorial it will seem more impartial.

Sponsorship is rather more long-term in its way of working than advertising and received wisdom has it that it is not the place for long messages. Well . . . maybe, but a company hiring heaters has made very effective use of motor rally sponsorship to say 'Andrews Heat for Hire'. Apart from brief messages like that, sponsorship can't really inform, although it can *persuade*, by building an image, by shifting perceptions and by simply reminding people that a company exists.

With the introduction of more and more magazines, newspapers, TV channels and so on, the fragmentation of the media means that there is an awful lot of clutter and it is difficult even to be seen or heard. Sponsorship can help because if the public relations side is handled properly, a well-constructed link can get coverage across a wide area; it can spread further than *promo*tion and help you to get noticed by creating *com*motion. And it is a flexible tool – you can sponsor almost anything from, say, a small booklet to a large brass band or, presumably, a battleship, and at a local, national or international level. Just as the scale is flexible so too is the form: you may sponsor individuals, groups, events or things and you have a wide selection from the arts, sport, the environment, etc.

With so many available permutations it is possible to target a sponsorship link as precisely as an ad, particularly if the activity sponsored has research figures about its audience. Sponsorship can reach very precise groups as well as very small ones and if you worked hard enough I am sure you could reach just left-handed fly-fishermen (someone probably already has).

Sponsorship can add spice to a company and rejuvenate an image by making it appear more dynamic. Sponsorship influences an image by 'lending' the image factors from the activity sponsored. For instance, show-jumping is perceived as high class and prestigious, rugby as strong and rugged, motor sport as exciting and international and so on. If you have a 'cold' image you could soften it by sponsoring a gentle, cosy activity.

Sponsorship can be particularly valuable for 'low-interest' products which people would really prefer not to have to buy, such as insurance. So if Harrisons sell insurance, having their banners at sponsored cricket matches, with a competition carrying their name, will project an image of calmness and stability; if our friends sell melons then 'Harrisons' melons' across the vests of nubile lady athletes may get them even more exposure. The degree of subtlety depends on the product and the sponsored activity, although ideally there needs to be some product or image connections for sponsorship to work really well. Above all, if it *is* to work well sponsorship must be carried through to point-of-sale, advertising and so on – it must be an integral part of a business plan, not something done in secret by consenting adults.

Sponsorship can pave the way before you start selling in a new territory and it can prepare the market for a new product launch because research shows that the more people have heard of your name, the more they will like you. And sponsorship can make you an active part of the local community; ideal for instance if you are opening a new branch and useful on an ongoing basis too – you may even attract better staff if you have a good local image through sponsorship. And remember, if you sponsor something, your competitors can't.

On a less savoury note, sponsorship may help if you are under attack, although it should have been started *before* the attack – if you sponsor something after coming under pressure it will be rather obvious why you are doing so. On a less savoury note still, sponsorship may even be a way of getting round laws prohibiting certain products from being advertised.

Consider a few specific things you may get from sponsorship:

- Media exposure. Sponsorship is now so much a part of the scene that the announcement of a sponsorship link should merit press attention as a story in its own right and, if you have chosen well, there should be ongoing opportunities to attract coverage.
- Employee interest if, for example, there is a team for people to follow. It is desirable (and it should be possible) to involve employees in almost any sponsorship.
- Name exposure at events through display banners, sponsors' names on participants' and supporters' clothing and so on.
- Your name incorporated in the title of an event.
- Special ticket allocations for you and your guests.
- Programme advertisements reserved for you, perhaps with competing products excluded.
- A peg for point-of-sale material.
- Promotional (and sales) opportunities with clothing, umbrellas and so on featuring the sponsorship link. If it rains at your outdoor event (it will), people putting up

umbrellas with your logos on them will stir your heart.
- Opportunities to involve customers with, for example, road shows touring retail outlets and featuring stars you are sponsoring.
- Longevity. Sponsorship can live on – if a star starts on his way in your junior championship this may well get mentioned for years in the press and through the resurrection of video footage.
- High level contacts. If you get to know people via sport or the arts you should find it easier to sell to them later.
- Sponsorship may offer things you or your customers simply could not obtain in any other way, such as a peep 'behind the scenes' (which everyone loves) at an artistic event.
- Perhaps most important of all, opportunities for entertaining people at the events you sponsor. Business really can be mixed with pleasure, often very profitably.

Lastly, sponsorship can actually be fun and, let's face it, business can be a bit of a grind at times. Money spent on sponsorship may give you more enjoyment (and better results) than the same amount spent on advertisements. The Monte Carlo Rally used to run a *concours d'élégance* for vehicles which were often extensively kitted out and one year a sanitary ware retailer sponsored a car and fitted a miniature bathroom in the back. I hitched a lift back from Monaco with the crew and, with some modest pride, suspect I am the only person who can claim to have travelled across France sitting on a lavatory. You wouldn't get the same thrill from placing an ad in *Plumbing and Heating*.

If nothing else, sponsorship will get people saying 'Who on earth is . . . ?' You'd never heard of old Harrison until a few pages ago, had you?

I hope I've convinced you that sponsorship offers enough for you to consider it as part of your marketing mix. But I shouldn't end the chapter on such a euphoric high because it isn't easy going and there are probably more dissatisfied sponsors around than advertisers.

Don't expect sponsorship to solve deep-rooted problems. It's a bit like public relations in that if you have a lousy product or a service problem, no amount of sponsorship will make the trouble disappear – in fact it could actually make things worse if customers consider you are wasting money on sponsorship which should be spent on R & D. The key is not to lose your business sense; vow not to get carried away. If you are offered a sponsorship link and are told in reverent tones that 'all sponsors' names will appear on a plaque in the foyer', don't genuflect and say 'gosh'. Pause instead and reflect whether there will be more worthwhile benefits.

The same realism is needed over entertaining. If you take company directors to the opera in evening dress, do recognize that what you are doing is no more or less than an upmarket extension of taking sales representatives to a nightclub. The only difference is that you won't need to sponsor the latter. Where would the strippers display your name anyway? Really.

Tosca or tassles – it's up to you. (The scratching sound you hear is my name being struck off the Glyndebourne mailing list.)

Chapter 3 **Planning**

If you now feel that sponsorship may have a role to play in your affairs, don't lurch into it and commit to the first project you are offered. Instead, pause and *plan*. And if the heavy emphasis on planning throughout this book bores you then I am sorry. But not very sorry (we already have your money) because planning may make the difference between success and failure and – to concentrate your mind as the executive in charge of sponsorship – even between your keeping or losing your job.

Organization

The first thing to do when planning to become a sponsor is to sort out your internal organization and find a proper home for sponsorship; whether you handle it in-house or through an agency, you need to be quite clear where final responsibility lies within the company. Sponsorship should not merely be the chairman's personal fief but a fully integrated part of a company's affairs. Responsibility for sponsorship may lie with the sales, marketing or advertising manager, with public or community affairs or, increasingly, with a special sponsorship executive. Many areas of a company will need to be consulted and involved in sponsorship but ultimately one (and only one) executive should be in control (it may be difficult to get this accepted in the early days because people will be tempted to tinker with the new toy). Make the effort to impose a clear organization to avoid confusion which could even lead to a crafty or lucky sponsorship-seeker playing one area of the company off against another. In general, the higher up the corporate tree sponsorship reports, the better it is likely to work. And although you will wish to analyse any project you are offered, do structure things so that you are able to make quick decisions.

A company starting mild sponsorship for the first time may decide not to hire an additional person but will just add the task to someone's job specification. If so, that 'someone' should be nominated before a company gets too involved in decision-making and, once appointed, it makes sense to route all requests to the company for support – whether from sportsmen or charities – to him or her. Yes, include charitable appeals too because although these may be treated differently at the moment, my guess is that they will increasingly be considered as 'mainstream' sponsorship. Having stressed that public relations should be closely consulted, it is perhaps worth pointing out that it is poor PR not to reply to requests for support although, amazingly, many companies fail to do so; when saying 'no', don't hold out false hopes in order to be kind if you have really no intention of aiding someone.

Incidentally, the person in charge of sponsorship will find that the Sponsorship Association exists to encourage its development and has some well-meaning aims; no doubt other groups will spring up in due course. You may find some advantage in being able to compare notes and avoid pitfalls by joining such associations, although if you are confident enough to operate in business without clinging to the various marketing and PR organizations for support (and were never very active in the Cubs or Brownies), you probably won't bother.

Policy

Once you have sorted out internal responsibility for sponsorship, move on to consider your overall strategy.

Decision-making about sponsorship tends to be a bit woolly and subjective at times but it shouldn't be and, to clarify your thinking, draw up a 'sponsorship policy' which sets out very simply the company's overall approach. For instance, consider such things as:

- Do you wish to concentrate on sport or the arts or the community, or are you prepared to consider anything? Similarly, do you wish to support individuals and/or organizations?
- Are you willing to contribute to general running costs and building funds or only to specific events?
- Are you prepared to consider hazardous activities? Some companies fight shy of them although I'm not convinced that if, say, a power-boat crashes any odium attaches to a featured sponsor. It might of course if a sponsored 'stunt'

was seen to be a tomfool idea which should never have been undertaken.

Different companies will have different things to consider or guard against but, once word gets around – as it will – that you are a potential sponsor, you will be glad of a clear policy because it will enable the decision-maker to eliminate many approaches quite quickly; a similar policy will be desirable for charitable appeals too as their number escalates. A simple company policy will also help you to resist some of the inevitable appeals you will get from customers or through the old boys' network; it is easier to say 'no' if you have a positive reason for doing so, such as 'Sorry we can't support your building appeal but we direct all our available funds to the handicapped.'

Objectives

Having thought through your broad-brush policy, next consider your specific objectives in using sponsorship. To do this you must know where you are trying to get to, because one thing is certain: if you are heading nowhere you are likely to reach your destination. But before you decide where you are trying to get to, you must know where you are *now*. If you want to use sponsorship to enhance your image, what attitudes do people currently have towards you? You don't know? Then how will you be able to tell if sponsorship works? I'm sure you see the point – you must have a feel for your present situation if sponsorship is to be effective; don't just do it because it gives you a nice warm feeling.

Consider your corporate strengths and weaknesses when drawing up objectives. Are you already a household name? If so, is your sheer size actually working to put people off you? In this case you may consider sponsoring something deliberately low-key, although if you *are* large do bear in mind that you should still go first class – you could confuse people if, say, as a first league credit card company you sponsor a fourth league sport (unless the team is based in the same town as your head office).

Is your image a bit dull and dowdy? Then you may consider sponsoring something up-to-date and exciting to brighten it. Is your image rather down-market? You may be able to raise it through sponsoring an activity with an expensive feel about it (even the Pope and some of the Royals now take sponsors' support – some would say regrettably).

If you wish to use a sponsored activity for entertaining customers, what sort of people are they and what would appeal to them? For that matter what is wrong with your present way of treating them? If hospitality is your main reason for sponsoring, bear in mind that several companies offer packages which include tickets to major sporting and artistic events with, say, an accompanying banquet at which stars (some a bit shopworn admittedly) are present. You will not need to be a formal sponsor to treat clients to these outgoings although there is always the risk that you will arrive at an event to find your key competitor is the main sponsor. Incidentally, you should always check carefully that such packages have the blessing of event organizers, otherwise you may find you have poor seats and a hospitality area miles away from the action.

Are you considering sponsorship to increase brand awareness . . . or improve community or employee relations . . . or, well, or countless other reasons? Just be clear what your particular objectives are, and do write them down.

By the way, set achievable objectives, won't you? If you have two sewing machinists working in your boxroom, sponsoring a local netball team may well raise local awareness of your company, but it would be unduly optimistic to set as an objective that the nation should drop its Marks and Spencer underwear to don yours. Which is perhaps an appropriate point to consider:

The brief

Having drawn up a sponsorship policy and considered your objectives, move on to draw up a detailed brief to help you select an appropriate activity to sponsor. The brief will become in effect a 'selection checklist' and the tighter it is the better the result will be for you, because the closer you will be able to match a sponsored activity to your needs. It is perhaps no coincidence that the most successful sponsors include banks and insurance companies whose natural instincts are to be precise in their approach. When drawing up your own individual brief (and it must be individual because every company has different needs) consider things like these:

1. Does the sponsorship offered comply with your policy and will it enable you to meet your objectives?
2. What target audience are you trying to reach? Does the project match?

3. Is TV exposure important? If so, will the activity attract it?
4. Are your aims short- or long-term? Will the timing of the activity fit in with the aims?
5. What promotional opportunities are you seeking? Will what you are offered provide them?
6. Is the activity unique or only one of many similar things on offer? If the latter, can it be given its own special personality?
7. Does the activity have a logical link with your company? If not, could one be forged?
8. Will it appeal to your key customers if you take them to events?
9. Can the project and your links with it be properly exploited?
10. Will your sponsorship gel with – or at the very least not conflict with – your usual advertising approach?
11. Will the link have any 'stretch' in it? In other words if your sponsorship is a success will you be able to broaden your connection in future years?
12. Is the activity already linked with a sponsor? If so be wary because the link may be hard to shift in people's minds.
13. Would the sponsorship be exclusive to you? Or would you be one of a crowd?
14. Do those involved have a serious approach to sponsorship? Or are they still in the Dark Ages, regarding sponsors as intruders?
15. Are any of those taking part personalities who, for instance, would pull people into your showroom or to your stand at an exhibition?
16. I hope hardbitten businessmen won't laugh but, when you stop sponsoring, will your efforts have left the particular activity a bit *better*? I'm not just being sentimental in asking you to consider this because, if you leave something worse off than when you started, you may well receive (and deserve) adverse publicity.
17. A final thought for your checklist – if you start sponsoring, what will your key competitor/s do? If you sponsor one racehorse, will they sponsor two? Will the public notice or care? Will it matter? Probably not.

You may well add specific points of your own to that list and you should then allow a certain flexibility in your final selection process otherwise you may miss an opportunity because it doesn't conform exactly to your brief. Three further key areas should be considered when drawing up any brief:

1. Geographical spread

How far do you hope to reach with your sponsorship? Do you want it to be local, regional, national or even international? At the moment around 60 per cent of sponsorship is aimed nationally with the balance spread between the rest. My feeling is that the mix will tend to polarize as satellite TV offers multinational scope to sponsors on the one hand, while on the other demands from the community will increase sponsorship activity at a local level. Whatever your particular needs, you should be able to find an activity which matches them.

If you are well known nationally, there may be a case for channelling sponsorship through your branches to help local community relations and soften the 'cold' image which a national reputation on its own may produce. When considering geographical spread, don't fall into the common trap of thinking that the world stops 30 miles from your head office. And if you are based in the south, remember that Watford isn't the gateway to the Tundra (or so I'm told).

If you decide to move on to the international stage (and it could be foolhardy to do so as your first effort) you will find far more glamour and impact, but these will be coupled with far more problems. There will be the complication of currencies and foreign languages while legal and media customs may be different (correction, *will* be different) and in addition it may be less easy to measure results than at home. You will need to allow far more time when planning and strong central coordination will be essential, with detailed briefing documents clearly spelling out who does what and when (and possibly to whom).

Don't assume practices will be the same as at home if you venture abroad.

Do watch the timing of any announcements – if you don't coordinate things properly, news may dribble out and dampen the impact.

Do take care in trying to impose sponsorship on local management abroad; if they are not consulted in advance they may kill it by indifference.

But don't let me put you off. Even in the richest countries people are seeking sponsorship and the opportunities for international links must grow.

2. Timing

This is the second area needing extra attention. Awareness of sponsorship is slow to build up but difficult to destroy, which is why you should be wary of taking over from an existing sponsor; it may even be better to leave an activity fallow for a year before picking it up if you are prepared to risk it still being available.

You should aim to sponsor for a minimum of three years and preferably five, although this will not be possible if, say, someone is planning to ski across the Channel on an ironing board. Although you may have to pull out quickly if a link goes sadly sour, you should avoid bobbing in and out of sponsorship and instead try to build a proper relationship and give it time to work.

Where the sponsored activity is in its own life cycle also needs thought. Fashions change in the arts and in sport (I profoundly regret the years I wasted mastering the Twist and the hoola-hoop) and if you are trying to update your image you should sponsor an activity which is on the way up, not one about to become passé. If you are aiming at the youth market it may be better to be one month early than one year late in your timing.

Although it may not be possible to achieve too great a degree of sophistication, keep your own timing needs in mind when forging a link. For instance, if your peak selling time is the run-up to Christmas, do you want your main burst of sponsorship activity to be when shops are selling to the public or earlier, when your reps are selling in to the shops?

3. Finance

Last, but clearly not least, on your list should be 'Will the sponsorship be cost-effective?' Here I have to leave you largely on your own because only you will be able to judge if sponsorship will be value for money for you. What percentage of your total promotional budget should be spent on sponsorship? I wouldn't presume to tell you. There is no 'recognized' figure (and ignore one if it is ever quoted to you by a marketing guru) because sponsorship is so flexible that there cannot be a norm. If you are a small company trying to make a name, spending 100 per cent of your promotional budget on sponsorship may make eminent sense; if you are a national company, devoting less than 1 per cent to local programmes may make equal sense. Have the courage to make your own decision; after all that's why you've got the key to the executive washroom and that slightly rheumy rubber plant.

Keep in mind that you don't necesarily have to outspend your competition; you may be able to time your sponsorship so that you get concentrated coverage at critical times or you may simply be able to outwit your rivals through a clever sponsorship link; flair needn't cost money.

If your funds would be stretched by undertaking a major sponsorship programme, you may consider becoming a joint sponsor, but take care. Be sure the other sponsor is a company you would wish to be linked with because if it hits problems during the agreement you are likely to be tainted by them. Even if you have all the funds you need, you may consider giving, say, a local newspaper an almost free ride as a joint sponsor with you because your coverage should then be guaranteed in at least one outlet (although other newspapers may be somewhat lukewarm).

Finally, a message for company finance men: much as it will undoubtedly cause them anguish, they should try to be flexible when handling sponsorship. Amateur arts and sports organizations (professional ones too for that matter) may not understand or be geared to cope with elaborate company systems; sponsorship will work best if you can swing something simple. Let me stress that, despite this stricture, I have the highest respect for bean counters and implicitly follow my own accountant's advice (although it isn't always easy living on the Isle of Dogs as a tax exile).

Chapter 4 **Deciding What to Sponsor**

Before setting out to select something to sponsor, you must decide just how significant TV coverage is to your plans. TV is obviously not quite as important as people perhaps suppose because only around 10 per cent of significant sponsorship links involve TV coverage. In fact, if TV exposure is the be-all and end-all of your life, perhaps you should be looking at a TV advertising campaign instead of sponsorship.

Do be a shade sceptical when appraising TV exposure for a proposed link. You may be quoted countless minutes (even hours) of TV exposure around the world for an activity, but consider carefully just how much of your name or logo is likely to be seen; if you happen to link with one of the also-rans in a particular sport (and even the best have off years), your exposure may be minimal as the cameras follow the pacemakers. And consider too the actual size of the viewing audience – it may not be all that high if the event you sponsor is televised at a poor time.

When evaluating the importance of TV, keep in mind that while it can certainly enhance an event by making it an 'occasion', it can also be a confounded nuisance if hospitality is really your main objective because an influx of TV people (and they often appear overmanned) can cause considerable interference with an event. And TV can disrupt in other ways: if one channel signs up the rights to a particular domestic activity, rival channels may concentrate on overseas events and lift their importance to an undeserved level. Conversely, if the TV rights to a major event are taken by an obscure cable TV company then, while the watching lighthouse keepers may enjoy the action, the event itself may suffer from (apparently) being downgraded.

All this assumes that TV will be clamouring to cover your event. In fact the reverse is far more likely to be the case and you and/or the sponsored activity will have to work hard to 'sell' the idea to TV companies, who may incidentally be more interested in a series than an isolated one-off event. Remember that live coverage is not always desirable for some activities which look more exciting with the boring bits edited out, and for this reason don't necessarily push for over-long TV coverage either. If a sport gets heavy TV coverage, this can even mar spectators' enjoyment of live events because they may miss the instant replays of key action which they get when watching at home.

If you try to negotiate TV coverage you will, whatever the channel, come up against various rules and, as a starter, it is important to appreciate the difference between a sponsored programme (covered in more detail in Chapter 8) and TV coverage of an event which is itself sponsored.

TV rules (which will depend on the company and may be un-written and subject to change) will govern how many credits (if any) you are likely to get on the captions plus how many mentions you will be given during a programme. Companies may draw a distinction between prime and other sponsors – they will not be prepared to credit endless sponsors on screen and in TV guides. As an aside, do you feel as I do that it looks and sounds incongruous when 'Mrs Emily Jones, wife of the deputy marketing manager of Harrisons' steps forward to present a trophy during a televised event?

The TV guidelines will also spell out the number of banners with which you will be allowed to decorate or desecrate the place; banners will not be allowed to come between the cameras and the action. Corporate identity specialists may be distressed to learn that TV companies may find logos more acceptable than names. Why? Because they don't believe the general viewer recognizes or understands such symbolism!

As far as perimeter advertising is concerned, TV companies recognize that they are guests (albeit often paying ones) at events and therefore cannot prevent it. However, lists of proposed advertisers have to be circulated before events relayed by the European Broadcasting Union and producers are warned to guard against last-minute dodges; as a sponsor you should avoid getting involved in tricks anyway, otherwise you will forfeit any goodwill for future occasions. Fluorescent or luminous adverts are banned because they may adversely affect the TV picture.

But don't be totally put off. TV companies may bend their hallowed rules (especially if they want an activity badly enough) and the more competition they face, the more flexible they are likely to become. However, if you do find a more relaxed attitude, be a shade cautious about putting any agreed rule bending in writing otherwise you may get adverse publicity in newspapers if letters are leaked (always assume they will be).

With, I hope, your thoughts now clarified about TV you can move on to consider:

What to sponsor

There is no need to panic because, although there may not be a tremendous selection at the national level (after all there are only a given number of national championships to sponsor), lower down the scale there is plenty of choice and, just to remind you yet again, it is a buyer's market. So if you attend a sports evening, don't let the bonhomie or Beaujolais lead you to agree to sponsor a fading boxer, and beware of the chief executive inflicting his personal enthusiasm for a particular art form on your customers – you need to be more objective in your decision-making. Beware too of automatically sponsoring something with which the company already has a mild connection (perhaps through someone's personal enthusiasm) because it may not be quite an ideal match for a more substantial arrangement. And be particularly cautious in sponsoring employees; I'm not saying you shouldn't, but do think things through carefully to avoid jealousies.

We will look at specific areas to sponsor over the next three chapters but, as a firm discipline, keep referring to your brief and do try to select an activity that has (or you can plausibly pretend has) a link with your products or aims.

Study the market segment to which the activity appeals, is it similar to the one you are trying to reach? Are the enthusiasts the right age and sex? If, as discussed in the previous chapter, you have decided what geographical spread you need, consider whether the things on offer match your aims. If you want regional coverage, don't sponsor an international affair with a price tag to match.

Play devil's advocate. 'Sponsors will be allowed to put their names on the transporter' may be quoted by supplicants from the showjumping world. How kind. But it could be cheaper to buy an old furniture van and have it driven up and down the M1 with 'Harrisons' Showjumping Team' painted on it. If you have any spare paint, make it the 'International' team to give yourself even more spurious glamour (don't actually buy any horses, of course). Far fetched? No – you can put your name on the side of taxis and that isn't sponsorship. It just illustrates that the individual components of a sponsorship package may not be all that great in isolation; your task will be to judge if the whole can be forged into something worthwhile.

Sponsorship works best if there is a genuine reason for the activity to happen, which is why 'manufactured' events are, in general, less successful than established ones for sponsors. With any sponsorship it does no harm if there are traces of patronage and doing good, which is why links with sporting charities and the like can be particularly effective. The most successful sponsorships have a uniqueness and a magic ingredient, such as a witty connection which helps along the press coverage.

Remember that some events become occasions in their own right, irrespective of the depth of public interest in the particular activity; most people would find a day at Ascot or Henley fairly bearable whether or not they were interested in horses or whatever it is they do at Henley. However, accept that it is practically impossible to get some events linked to a sponsor – for example, the Monte Carlo Rally will always be 'the Monte' to enthusiasts, irrespective of what name a sponsor tries to inflict on it. Don't waste your money on a similarly uphill conversion task.

Exactly what you sponsor may depend to some extent on how brave and innovative you are as a company. If you are prepared to be a pioneer and sponsor something new, well bear in mind that the risks will be greater with an activity which is still settling down, and you may come unstuck, but if it works you will be seen to be bold and venturesome. The growth of sponsorship means that so many avenues have been tramped that it is difficult to be unique but take care that the search for something special doesn't make you strain too hard – for instance, if you are considering an already heavily sponsored arena, you may have to struggle so much to find something to get you noticed that it would be better to look to another activity instead.

If, as is likely, you are faced with a choice of items to sponsor, try to mark the things on offer, weighting the areas which are of particular significance to you – employee interest, hospitality facilities or whatever. Even then the final decision may be a matter for business judgement (and why not?). One consolation: if you take a pricing decision and sales fall, your error will be obvious; if you choose the wrong one of several things to sponsor, few people will look back in anger.

One key decision you will face will be whether to sponsor sport, the arts or 'others'. In general, sport is good for mass audiences and to some extent the sponsorship may become an extension of your advertising. The arts tend to be more upmarket, with more overtones of social responsibility and there are fewer overriding national organizations controlling (or trying to control) affairs than sport.

Others? Anything else you can think of from conservation to community projects. Such projects will often have even stronger elements of good citizenships than the arts; there will be some tremendous opportunities in this field as sponsors and the sponsored learn to work with each other.

If you find your selection difficult then, all other things being equal, keep the following in mind:

- Does the activity you are considering have good management and good media links? It will be easier for you if it does.
- You will be much less at risk if you sponsor at the grass roots level rather than at the top of, say, a sport. Although the media mileage will be less, so will the fee.
- Consider how often an activity happens. If you get an annual event wrong, you've blown it, whereas if something occurs every fortnight or so you've got time to learn by your mistakes.
- If media exposure is important, whether a sport is dirty or clean will affect how well your name is displayed. Whether the activity happens in summer or winter, indoors or outdoors also needs consideration.
- Avoid areas where your competitors are already highly active. The sight of chairmen trying to beat each other via their boats or racehorses can become unappealing, especially to shareholders.
- The public tend to support the underdog, the young or the old (no-one cares for middle-aged authors). Women in what are supposed to be men's activities will also attract attention provided they are not seen to be simply gimmicks.

Finally, do watch out for political problems. Cowardly? Maybe, but unless you are deliberately seeking controversial coverage, why take the risk? Incidentally, I keep using the singular for the sponsored thing. You may be reckless or brave and sponsor several areas; I wouldn't in your first year but, if you do, maintain the same objective approach when selecting each one and then look for synergy between them.

How to find something

When entering the sponsorship world, keep an eye on magazines, newspapers and TV for opportunities, and do watch for trends so that you clamber on to a bandwagon before it has gathered too much speed. Contact the national associations of the activities you are considering sponsoring – the brighter ones may maintain a list of opportunities; read *Sponsorship News* for a spell to see what other companies are up to, and attend any sponsorship conferences and exhibitions (a growth area).

However, I suspect that all this may well be unnecessary because you will be approached directly by individuals, teams and event organizers, as well as by sponsorship agents, which we will consider in the next chapter.

Chapter 5 **Agents and Agencies**

If you have not been approached by sponsorship agents or agencies already, you certainly will be if word gets around that you are a potential sponsor (an 'agent' is likely to be purely a broker; an 'agency' will offer a full range of services). However, despite the growth in the number of such companies, it is believed that only around one-fifth of deals are done through them and they are not yet as established, or perhaps as trusted, as advertising agencies. Nevertheless, if you are new to sponsorship you should certainly consider using an agent to take on part or all of the work for you to save hiring extra staff; you could, for instance, consider contracting out the hospitality side or the preparation of a regular news bulletin on your sponsorship link.

You may consider using an agency for a year or so while you get the feel of sponsorship before handling it in-house, although this would be a somewhat churlish route if the company did all the work in creating a successful programme for you.

Do be cautious when selecting an agency. Standards vary widely: some are awful (perhaps because sponsorship is expanding so fast that there are not enough bright people to go round), others are highly efficient and sound business people.

Sponsorship is still a growth area and do remember that no qualifications are needed to set up as an agent or agency. No doubt meaningful codes of practice will emerge for them but they will need treating with the same scepticism as many similar codes. In the meantime, let the commissioning company beware.

When searching for someone to act for you in finding and operating sponsorship, ask around fellow businessmen, watch the ads in the marketing magazines and consult the national organizing bodies of the activities you are thinking of supporting because some of them maintain lists of sponsorship and PR companies offering specialized services. Tell your advertising agency what you are up to; they may not be wildly enthusiastic to see funds being diverted from mainstream advertising but, if they have a link with an agency, it may be worth considering that one because they will have more to lose if things start going sour.

When you have the names of two or three agencies ask them to make a presentation about themselves to you, preferably on their premises so that you can see what they are like; spell out what you hope to achieve through sponsorship and roughly what you plan to spend and then ask them to come back with recommendations. Be wary if they try to push you into a particular activity at your first meeting – you really need a more analytical approach.

When vetting companies, keep the following in mind:

- You must have a clear idea of what you are hoping to achieve, otherwise you won't be able to brief agents properly. Also be clear on what you want them to do – simply to find a project for instance, or also to administer it for you.
- Ask to see their client list. Do they work for any of your competitors? It may not necessarily be a problem but you should at least be aware of the potential conflict.
- Take up any references you are given. Check how long agencies have been in business, vet their track record and, of course, find out if they are solvent!
- Look at any promotional material the agency has prepared for its clients. Does it seem effective?
- Are the agencies well run? How do they handle the phone? Do they call back when they've promised? Do they reply to letters quickly? Do they appear to have done background research on your company? In other words, do they seem efficient?
- Ask to meet the people who will be working on your account if they win it – they may not be the ones who make the initial pitch for your business. *Will you be able to get on with them?* This is probably the single most important thing if the link is to work. At times an agent will need to be an 'interpreter' or interface between sponsor and sponsored and it is vital for you to feel that they are people you can trust. Check also just how many employees an agency has and whether they will have the capacity to handle your affairs.
- Do the agencies specialize in the area you are likely to be sponsoring? It will not always be essential that they have prior experience and contacts, but it is desirable that you

should both not be climbing a learning curve at the same time.

- Do the agencies offer the range of services you need – print facilities, press service and so on? Vet their claims: do they do such work in-house or simply know who to phone to get it done? And do they have the geographical spread you need, such as connections in other countries if you plan sponsorship at an international level?

Finally, when you have selected someone, be absolutely clear on the financial arrangements and don't forget to build appropriate items into your budget.

All the above assumes that you are appointing an agency to act for you just as you would an advertising agency or PR consultancy. However, it is more likely that you will be approached by an agent with something to sell on behalf of a sport or other activity. Even in this case you may still need someone to act for you, because a company which sells you something may not necessarily be the best one to operate and promote it for you (although, not unnaturally, they may well hope to do just that).

Although it may appear less than ideal to have an apparent conflict of interest with an agency acting for both sides of a deal, it can in fact sometimes work well because the agency will know just what each side can and can't do; it is illegal for an agency to take commission from both parties incidentally unless the arrangement has been disclosed to them. Normally if you are buying into something you will not pay an agent because his commission (which may vary from 10 to 25 per cent) will be paid by the sponsored activity.

If any agent approaches you, be absolutely clear which parties he is representing and what power he has. Above all, check that an agent really can *deliver* what he is promising, otherwise you may find that you are tangled with someone who is juggling to put a package together and needs your commitment to make the other balls fall into place.

As you get embroiled in sponsorship you may find managers entering the fray on behalf of sports stars and the like. If they, or agents themselves for that matter, expect too much say and sway, show them the door; a small but I suspect increasing number of sponsors are refusing to deal with activities where managers try to intercede on behalf of participants. Never forget it is a buyer's market. Things can also get a shade uneasy if agents are handling, say, sportsmen as well as sporting events because there can be a pull of priorities; it may get even sleazier if journalists (who are supposed to be impartial) are handling PR for participants.

The message is simply that, while agents and agencies can be useful, you should not lose your normal business sense when dealing with them even if they do impress you by appearing to be on first name terms with the stars. And if an agent selling a package approaches you like 007 with a licence to over-kill with high-falutin' phrases implying that you would be an idiot not to sign up at once, fire back some low-falutin' ones of your own. Like 'What will I get for the money?'; 'Is that all?'

And 'Goodbye'.

Chapter 6 Sports

Despite inroads by the arts, sport still takes the lion's share of sponsorship; it is brasher than the arts and, partly because of that brashness, there are fewer pitfalls for the sponsor, particularly over matters of good taste. And sport gets far greater TV exposure than the arts, not least because television companies have at least to pretend that sport is important because it may be a relatively cheap form of programming for them; as a result, some sports may get more TV exposure than the real public interest in them perhaps warrants.

Because of the sheer volume of sports sponsorship, the law of diminishing returns may apply for sponsors struggling to be heard above the clamour. To increase the chances of getting value, it is essential that companies take care to tailor the sports sponsored to their target audiences. Sweeping generalizations can be misleading, but let's try a few: athletics have a broad spectrum of appeal; cricket appeals mainly to men; horse racing is green and relaxed, although the jockeys usually look sickly, while darts players look bloated; boxing has a poor image yet is widely used for client entertaining by some business segments. Anyway, whatever image you crave, you should be able to find a sport to help you achieve it.

Although sponsoring any sport should help you to reach the opinion formers in the particular activity (via enthusiast magazines and so on), there may be major differences in what exposure you can get to wider audiences at the events themselves via banners etc; consider the difference between motor sport, where anything goes, and Wimbledon tennis which is slightly more genteel. Incidentally, although people make much of the importance of sports ground advertising, I will just note in passing that a growing body of advertising opinion questions just how cost-effective it is. Back to backing your business judgement.

If you plan to sponsor sport, you need to decide at an early stage just how important it is that you back winners. Success on the field or track is not essential to all sponsorship but in general people do like to be involved with winners; certainly the press will give them more coverage than also-rans. Should a sponsor get too closely associated with a jolly good loser, the company itself may be seen as just that: a loser. If you can't find a potential winner then go for something unique in other ways, such as the likely best British or Welsh competitors, to ensure you get adequate coverage.

There are believed to be around 150,000 sports clubs in the UK, of which 110,000 are affiliated to various governing bodies. It all looks very organized. However, you will find wide differences in the levels of efficiency of the governing bodies. Some will have a firm grip and be aware of developments in sponsorship (and opportunities available) while others will be hopelessly out of touch; beware of sports where the administrators are still struggling to get to grips with the wireless let alone sponsorship. The brighter organizing associations (many of whom will be implementing the rules of an international body) will have detailed information available to potential sponsors about the numbers, ages and sex of spectators for instance; some may have off-the-shelf packages on offer, extending to tickets, badges, T-shirts, stickers and so on. However, be clear exactly what you are getting with such packages because some may simply be advertising or entertaining deals, available to all and sundry, rather than sponsorship which should entail closer involvement.

At an early stage of negotiation you should establish if the person or body you are dealing with is linked to a regional or national organization. 'Pirate' associations spring up in some sports (often where the national bodies have not kept in touch with younger members) but these can present problems for sponsors with, for instance, squabbles and household names prohibited from participating. Be wary even with more organized sports if the sportsmen and the organizing bodies are quarrelling – you may get caught in the crossfire. Happily, one cause for controversy, the agonizing over who is or isn't an amateur, is fading because as costs rise barriers tumble and most sports are becoming 'open'. And how times have changed, with today's 'gentleman' player more likely to ask the 'professional' for his autograph than to direct him to the tradesmen's entrance.

A few general points about sports sponsorship:

1. Even in such a cluttered field, a novel sponsorship, such as

so much per goal for a team or so many pounds of meat for a weightlifter, will get media coverage.

2. If you decide to pay partly by results, be clear if you wish to reward just the top few or spread your largesse through the ranks. Even if you concentrate on the leaders, don't neglect the lower reaches entirely because there may be a lot of goodwill to be gained there at low cost. (Some sportsmen seem unwilling to plough anything back into the sports that made them famous and rich – but you needn't be so shortsighted.)

3. Without making things confused, remember that the more sections, groups or categories you have, the more opportunities there will be for media mentions and photographs of 'winners'. It will be even better if some geographical spread can be introduced among the winners to widen the coverage.

4. Be clear what visibility you want in sponsoring sport. If you sponsor a balloonist you should be happy with the space available for your logo; there may be fewer opportunities with chess players, for instance.

5. Consider picking up an unknown or oddball sport, if you think it has potential, and making it thine. Mind, do check first just why it has been unsponsored; maybe there are snags you've missed.

6. Don't expect sportsmen to be gifted public speakers. Some are superb and by all means encourage others to learn enough to cope with the press and to say a few words at a sales conference, but don't expect to totally remodel what you've 'bought'.

7. Encourage sportsmen to be ambassadors for your company but discourage them from plugging your products so much that it becomes off-putting and causes the media to shy away. Mind, I hope you fare better than a car dealer who loaned a car to a star who was later asked at a public forum what sort it was. 'I think it's a blue one' was the languid reply. I'm not suggesting he should have given chapter and verse on the number of cylinders or eulogised about the seating (that would have been counter-productive) but . . . let's just say the sponsorship wasn't renewed.

Individuals

Supporting a single sportsman is probably the highest risk area in sports sponsorship because an injury or a spell off form or even a temperamental outburst may damage your investment. Nevertheless many such links are successful when both sides pull their weight. But care is needed: for instance, if you sponsor just one member of a team this may create jealousy among the others which will rebound against you. If you support a sportsman in his formative years, don't expect him to be loyal to you if he reaches the top; you may be lucky but the chances are that, sooner rather than later, an agent or manager will blow in his ear and lead him off to richer sponsors.

Don't be overawed by reputations when negotiating individual sponsorship. If it is stated that a sponsorship fee buys you a given number of days of a star's time, decide *before* signing what use you will be able to make of that time. If, say, the fee is £5000 and the going rate for an appearance by a star of his calibre is £500 then you need around 10 appearances to justify the investment; are you *sure* you can really use him that often without hitting overkill?

Just as you may pay by goals, runs or whatever, so you could relate the sponsorship fee for an individual to the level he (and, if I haven't mentioned it before, most of the 'hes' in this book could of course be 'shes') reaches in his particular sport – pay him more, say, if he is selected for a national team; it should be value because media interest in him will increase.

Finally, if you wish to sponsor an individual, remember you may be able to select one with a non-speaking role, such as a greyhound or horse, but do check if the prevailing rules will allow you to use your selected name for the beast *before* you sign the contract.

Teams

You will be on slightly safer ground if you sponsor a team but you should still be clear just what you are buying; check if any of the team members already have personal sponsors which could lead to clashes with your requirements. And do the rules of the sport allow team clothing to feature your name or logo?

Events

If you sponsor an event you are on probably the safest ground of all because, provided it is efficiently organized, you will not be affected by who wins. But note: efficiently organized. Are the proposed organizers in control of their destiny? Are they efficient? How successful was their last event? Did they keep proper records? Ask to see their books (but don't expect to find highly systematized records if it is a small amateur group).

As with individuals and teams, before sponsoring an event do establish exactly what you are getting and check, for instance, that there are no problems removing existing advertisements from a ground for your proposed event. Keep in mind an earlier point about the difficulty of getting the name of an established event switched to yours, while if you are asked to sponsor a newly created event (perhaps simply designed to trap a sponsor like you) then do establish if there is a real need for it in the sport; don't inflict it on the world otherwise. Be particularly wary of created *non*-events such as nude snooker (give them time) or alcohol-free darts (less likely) because the top stars may not be permitted to take part if the contests are not sanctioned by their national body. Even if the stars can participate, they may just go through the motions and not try, thus cheating both you and the spectators.

Instead of sponsoring an event with your name in the title, you may decide instead to be an 'official supplier' of whatever keeps the wolf from your door, but do accept that you may have to work hard to get noticed. Naturally, if you are providing technical equipment, and advertising the fact, then it does need to function properly – during one World Cup newspaper ads were trumpeting the high-tech TV equipment in use just when viewers were kicking their sets at the low-tech results.

Despite the pitfalls, the opportunities for sports sponsorship are endless. If you sponsor an event or championship you could extend the association by sponsoring the top few as they move to higher levels . . . you could sponsor just one corner of a racetrack or one jump of a racecourse or the corner post at a boxing match (although in isolation these would be advertising) . . . you could have your logo on a boxer's dressing gown or, if less confident, on the soles of his shoes. Or . . . well, it's up to you.

Fortunately, as you face the bewildering choice there is help at hand.

The *Sports Council* is the executive body and the specialist agency for sport in Britain. Although it is an arm of the government, it is an independent one in the value judgements it makes. The Council puts forward a plan and, with luck, the government provides grants on the basis of that plan, the aim being to see mass participation in sport.

The Sports Sponsorship Advisory Service is a free service run by the Sports Council to help companies interested in sponsorship. For example, it produces lists of companies that have been identified as offering specialized services in sports sponsorship and it also has a booklet showing who sponsors what. The Sports Council for Northern Ireland, the Sports Council for Wales and the Scottish Sports Council offer similar services; the latter for instance produces an excellent newsletter of sponsorship leads.

The Central Council of Physical Recreation, or CCPR, is a confederation of over 200 governing bodies of sport and recreation; an umbrella organization if you like.

The Institute of Sports Sponsorship, administered by the CCPR, is a national non-profit making organization formed to encourage sponsorship and improve the understanding of it. It is intended to be a standing forum for people involved or interested in the sponsorship of sport.

Finally, to complete the picture, the *Sports Aid Foundation* is an independent organization (with the recognition of, among others, the Sports Council and the CCPR who are represented on the Board of Governors) which assists with the expenses of non-professional individual competitors who are preparing for certain specified major competitions. Sorry – they don't make grants to people training to be sponsors.

Onward, ever onward.

Chapter 7 The Arts

With the growth of sponsored 'junk' sports, specifically created for TV, some would argue that in turning to the arts we are now moving from the ridiculous to the sublime. Whatever your views, you will be less at risk as a sponsor in the arts world than with sport, although your media mileage may be less.

Attitudes to sponsors in the arts field are more important than sheer *awareness* of them; it may be difficult to get heavy media coverage and name exposure to shift awareness, but a stylish and relaxed evening (for instance, at a theatre) may be an excellent and safe way of reaching key decision-makers among your customers and improving their attitude to you. The arts world has a more 'quality' image than sport with many audiences and it is an area where, happily, sponsorship will carry overtones of good citizenship and improving the quality of life. People may be bored at a ballet (you are? Welcome to Philistines Anonymous) but they will somehow feel it is good for them (rather like eating muesli) and the halo effect will be useful for the sponsor.

But life isn't perfect and nor is the world of arts sponsorship. The relationship between government and the arts tends to be a bit stormy; however it trumpets about freedom, a government's natural inclination may be to control whereas art needs freedom to flourish and if slanging matches are going on a sponsor may get caught in the middle. The bickering may extend to whether support should be concentrated on major activities in London or spread wider, while the major battles may be over the actual amount of government funding. Leading figures in the arts world hardly help their case by their arrogant assumption that the country simply *must* support the arts (and them, of course) in the style to which they should perhaps never have become accustomed. There is a counter view that if, say, an opera cannot put enough bums on seats to be viable then the bums on stage should lower their fees, and that if more effort was put into CAD-CAM than Carmen, in the long term the country would be healthier and thus better able to subsidize the arts.

Art will not give you the same visibility as sport because, for example, TV is less likely to keep giving name plugs, which could be seen as in bad taste anyway if overdone. And some critics will see art as elitist and maybe irrelevant; however enlightened your employees are, I think I'd be cautious about announcing an opera sponsorship the week before tough wage negotiations with people who perhaps wouldn't know their arts from their elbows. For the same reason you must be cautious in making judgements on the tastes of the masses. Trust your own judgement, of course – it's what you are paid for – but seek advice too and watch that your search for good taste doesn't become so refined that you receive no publicity at all for your money. Conversely, don't go overboard in the other direction and change the name of the sponsored thing to increase your coverage; an opera called the 'Hair Stylist of Seville' would be going too far, even if sponsored by a unisex salon. Almost as bizarre, don't let company executives demonstrate their talents at sponsored events, no matter how well they were received in school concerts (it has happened).

If you search for advice about arts sponsorship, you will find fewer and less clear-cut layers of control than in sport, which of course is no bad thing, although there are still some organizations to assist you. Briefly, the Grand Fromage is the Arts Council of Great Britain which receives funds from the Office of Arts and Libraries. The Council is allegedly 'independent' but its members are appointed by government and all its funds come from that source so how independent it is is open to conjecture. The theory is that the Council should be a buffer to prevent direct government interference in the arts.

The Arts Council in turn distributes largesse (all paid by us the taxpayers, of course) via regional arts associations; there are 13 of these in England plus three in Wales, although none in Scotland because the Scottish Arts Council acts in that role. There is a view that Britain needs a more embracing body, perhaps even a Ministry of Culture, but I'm not convinced – I don't know how you measure our quality of life but I suspect the muddle and huddle make a not insignificant contribution to it. However, three political parties say they would abolish the Arts Council or make drastic changes to it so shifts in the scene seem certain in the long term.

Arts organizations being subsidized should not receive more than 40 per cent of their needs from government; they have to make up the rest from ticket sales and other activities, like sponsorship, which is why you should be assured of a warm welcome. However, there are still arts activities around which may think they have a divine right to your funds. You will disabuse them, won't you? Note by the way that I am not using a capital 'A' for arts, we should not take them *that* seriously, nor should you let the high priests distract you from your main business aims – read your brief again.

If you are considering a modest local sponsorship, your first point of call in your search for something to sponsor (assuming you haven't found anything from the cascade of appeals through the post) could be to a local or regional arts association. The officials may have pet axes to grind but they may also be able to point you in appropriate directions and highlight potential problem areas.

If you then aspire to something more significant, to help you there is the Association of Business Sponsorship of the Arts (ABSA). This is in effect a trade association of businesses interested in arts sponsorship. The Association publishes a quarterly bulletin and keeps a register of sponsorship opportunities as well as a computer list of members. Sensibly, they advise arts organizations that they cannot register their projects unless they include a list of benefits to sponsors. ABSA also organizes an annual awards scheme (sponsored by the *Daily Telegraph*) with recognition of the best corporate programme, best first-time sponsor and so on.

Perhaps most significantly of all, ABSA administers BSIS on behalf of the Minister of the Arts. I'm sorry about all the initials but BSIS is the Business Sponsorship Incentive Scheme, under which the government matches first-time sponsors' money on a pound for pound basis provided the amount is over £1000; if existing sponsors increase their commitment then the government chips in £1 for every £3 from the sponsor, provided the new sponsorship is over £3000. There is an upper limit of £25,000 in either case. Naturally the hope is that if a new sponsor is tempted by this scheme, he will stay involved. The scheme is selective, there is no guarantee that an award will be made, and payment is only made to bona fide arts organizations who must be registered charities or non-profit distributing companies (are there any other sort in the arts?). Anyway, if you are interested, ABSA have an explanatory leaflet on the scheme with a simple form to be completed.

In America by the way, the Business Committee for the Arts

serves a similar role to ABSA and produces extremely high quality material to help its members.

Having sought all the advice you can, here are a few general points (and one vital one) to consider when deciding what to sponsor in the arts:

- Even if the area you are sponsoring *wants* to work to give you high visibility, temper their charming approach with caution because the result may jar with the public and make you seem gauche. If the plugs for a sponsor are so heavy that they mar the enjoyment of an event then that is extremely poor PR.
- Be clear from the start how long you plan, or hope, to be a sponsor. Headlines reading 'Theatre goes dark as Harrisons withdraw sponsorship, accuses manager' may not be quite the curtain call you were seeking.
- Remember that your commercial skills should, in theory anyway, be better than an amateur group's at promotion and pulling in people to events like art exhibitions. So use them.

The one vital point is that you must steel yourself *not to interfere* with the integrity of the artists. If you sponsor a theatre, don't force them to perform only 'safe' plays; if you sponsor an art gallery, don't ban them from exhibiting avant-garde works. If a sponsored activity proposes an event which makes you shudder, leave them to it, but consider an educational programme to explain to the public and employees (not least yourself perhaps) just what the artist is groping towards. If a link with an artistic activity goes hopelessly wrong, as it may, you may simply have to extricate yourself but, in doing so, try not to be seen as a censor.

Opportunities for arts sponsorship are endless but, by way of illustration, if you decide to get involved with *music* you can sponsor artists, festivals (from jazz up or down according to taste) and tours, with tickets, posters, venues and so on carrying your name and logo. As a follow-up, or a separate project, records can be sponsored. Featured music can be carried over into other marketing campaigns and you may even be able to arrange lunchtime concerts for employees. Some unusual spin-offs may result; at the end of a factory concert by a famous orchestra, a wag shouted 'Do you do weddings?'. This not only sent everyone, including the musicians, away with a smile but also made a diary piece for newspapers.

One clear advantage with music is that it is possible to target an audience fairly precisely, and don't forget music can be fun – more so perhaps than some grunt and groan sports with bickering stars.

Similar opportunities occur if you support the *theatre*. If you are of a nervous disposition then check in advance that you will not be backing extremist productions to avoid the censorship problem mentioned earlier. Conversely, if you want a way-out image you may deliberately seek out such productions, while if you want to appear a cosy, family concern you could back a local pantomime and run schools competitions and so on in the run-up to the first night.

Art collections are perhaps a less obvious sponsorship area than music or the theatre, but the numbers are growing. As an example, one-third of the largest American corporations now have art collections or collect art (perhaps because, unlike the UK, purchases of works of art are tax-deductible there). They improve the work environment (some reckon you can tell the likely size of a lawyer's fee by the paintings on his walls) and, to gladden the hearts of accountants, can even be good investments, to the extent that security must be considered for such collections.

You may of course run the same risk with modern art as with avant-garde plays, but if someone stands with his finger in his ear, or anywhere else for that matter, and maintains it is 'art', who are you to gainsay him? Try explaining cricket to an intelligent person who has never heard of it, and is sober at the time.

Incidentally, if you sponsor an art collection, don't keep it to yourself – give the local community access to it.

You could sponsor a competition for the design of a magazine to help a local society, you could sponsor a poem, you could sponsor . . . well, you could sponsor whatever you wish in the arts; the more novel, the more mileage you may get. Just be sure that whatever you do is done for sound business reasons and meets your brief.

Chapter 8 Other Opportunities

As well as sport and the arts, there are countless other opportunities for sponsorship because almost *anything* can be linked to a sponsor in some way. The only limiting factor may be your imagination, otherwise the sky's the limit.

Television

And talking of sky, it is perhaps appropriate to start with TV, which is going through many changes. With DBS (direct broadcasting by satellite), cable TV, round-the-clock programmes and other developments, viewers should have much more choice and, in theory, it should be possible for companies to reach very small as well as very specific target audiences. A marketing man's dream? Perhaps. But the hype is running way, way ahead of the reality at the moment and many plans have come unstuck. One thing does seem certain however: there will be a great need for programmes to fill all the airtime in future years. Step forward sponsors because, whether called 'corporate underwriting', 'co-funding' or 'funding by non-broadcasters', plain and simple sponsorship of programmes themselves should have a growing part to play.

At the moment in Britain the BBC's Charter and the Broadcasting Act prohibit sponsored programmes on BBC and IBA services, with certain exceptions. The IBA guidelines are included as Appendix 1 if you wish to study them in detail but clause 4 covers the important exceptions:

> Acknowledgements to other funders will only be considered when the programme consists, in the terms of the Broadcasting Act, of a factual portrayal of doings, happenings, places or things. This includes recordings or live relays of sporting, artistic and entertainment events which have an existence independent of the television broadcast itself. It may also include documentary programmes, but is not to be taken as including (i) programmes on matters of political or industrial controversy or relating to currrent public policy, or (ii) news programmes.

They have in mind items which in the opinion of the IBA are proper for inclusion by reason of their intrinsic interest or instructiveness and do not comprise an undue element of advertisement.

Things are somewhat more relaxed on cable TV because the Cable and Broadcasting Act, 1984 permits sponsorship funding on cable programme services and requires the Cable Authority to issue a Code of Practice governing its conduct; this is included in Appendix 2 and is worth study if you are considering television sponsorship because cable TV could be a useful area in which to experiment at (relatively) low cost.

However, forget codes and guidelines for a moment because it isn't quite as cut and dried as all that, and just as TV companies try to adopt a realistic attitude to coverage of sponsored events, the same flexibility is likely to apply to sponsored programmes. It seems certain that commercial pressures will lead to opportunities for sponsors on even the most purist channels, while the more resourceful TV (and radio) companies have sponsorship units specifically to exploit new opportunities.

But what are the advantages in sponsoring a TV programme? These for instance:

- You can reach very specific target audiences. TV companies have detailed audience research figures – more sophisticated information than is available for many other areas of sponsorship.
- Programme sponsorship can give you a 'presence' and you may gain stature by doing it.
- If you select a programme with care you should be able to create the right environment to hawk your wares.
- You should receive a given number of name and product mentions.
- If you sponsor an actual programme, rather than simply advertise in one, there is less chance of people missing your message (as they may if they switch channels to avoid the ads).
- You can become involved with things which it would be difficult to sponsor or be associated with in any other way, for instance a documentary on a particular issue.
- Programmes may have a long life through repeats.
- Links can be arranged with station celebrities for personal appearances; competitions can be run and back-up material, such as booklets, produced.

However, despite those attractions, just as sponsorship is at the more exotic edge of marketing, so programme sponsorship is at the outer reaches of sponsorship itself and if you decide to go ahead I suggest you consult specialists in the field because this is less of a DIY area than more conventional branches of sponsorship. It is really a lot closer to pure advertising – in time I guess sponsorship will be divided into 'active' and 'passive', depending on the degree of direct involvement through such things as customer entertaining.

You will need to be very creative to get value and you must link with the right programme so that the audience matches your needs; keep your objectives firmly in mind.

If you are approached by someone with a proposal for a sponsored programme, do check carefully that there is actually a confirmed outlet for it, and remember to protect your interest in any ancillary rights – if your humble little programme becomes a world hit, you should be riding the gravy train too.

All hi-tech and glamorous? Maybe, but there are risks, for example:

1. It is possible to put people off you by being too intrusive. The risks of an over-rich brown voice announcing that 'this programme is brought to you by the makers of . . .' are too obvious to need stating aren't they? Then why are such apparent parodies still heard?
2. Relations with the TV company may not be easy. Some producers will react violently to outside pressures and the better the TV company, the worse co-producer it may be; some may want your money but no interference. You wouldn't dream of trying to interfere? Pull the other one.
3. There is some public concern about sponsored programmes. You and the producers may want to be fair in a programme, you may actually *be* fair . . . but people may still wonder what was left out. Even though the sponsor is named it doesn't remove the possibilities for distortion and critics fear that the sponsors' urge to interfere will be irresistible.
4. There is also concern over 'infomercials', that is commercials wrapped up (with varying degrees of subtely) as information programmes, especially where they reach children. Lines get somewhat blurred and you as a sponsor may appear a shade underhand (you may not be bothered, of course, as kids clamour for your wares).

All in all, sponsored TV programmes are an area where you need your wits and wallet about you. I will continue to peruse my collected works of Charles Dickens (unexpurgated) and watch developments with interest.

Radio

Like TV, radio is going through a sea change over sponsorship and the opportunities for sponsors will increase. Although radio does not cross international frontiers quite like TV, it costs a whole lot less and you have the flexibility of going local, network or part network.

The guidelines for sponsorship of radio programmes are much the same as for TV, with the emphasis again on 'the factual portrayal of doings, happenings, places or things'. This means you should be able to link with programmes about music festivals, quizzes, traffic reports by spotter planes (although attitudes to these seem to vary among stations), football match commentaries and so on.

You will find the warmest welcome if a strapped-for-cash radio station (and many of them are) simply couldn't make a programme without your support (in such cases you may become a co-producer). Because of financial pressures, the guidelines about sponsoring radio programmes will be under constant review and, for example, it is now possible to add 'a descriptive phrase' to a sponsor's acknowledgements.

Independent companies tend to be more relaxed about sponsorship than the BBC, while if you wish to experiment with radio sponsorship at low cost, community stations, covering a very small area, could be the place for you in the future, and should offer possibilities for the local businessman.

If I haven't put you off radio (and I recognize there will be plenty of consultants eager to put a counter view to switch you on) what are you likely to get for your money? Well, a sponsorship package is likely to include a given number of on-air mentions both during the programme and in trailers for it (you will improve your coverage chances if your name forms part of the programme title). You should also receive credits in programme guides and you will be able to co-operate over support materials – books, wallcharts or whatever. To further reinforce what you are doing, you can organize special events with appearances by local radio personalities (who, although perhaps unheard of a few miles away, may have a surprising local pull). And you should be able to book ads in the commercial breaks of the programmes you sponsor, although these should not be linked in style or context to the actual programme (a decidedly grey area).

However relaxed the rules become, there will of course always be some restrictions on what you can do (the broadcasters will want to keep control out of your hands) and such restrictions are in your own interests anyway – you could annoy listeners by overkill.

Films and video

There are various ways in which you can be involved with films and video, which are linked together here for convenience, although keep in mind that while it is possible to convert film to video, the reverse process is at present less satisfactory.

'Product placement' through which you ensure that your product, not a rival's, is shown on screen (for a fee) is sometimes described as sponsorship although it is perhaps closer to pure sales promotion. If lovers are groping on screen in a greenhouse I am not certain what impact it will have on your sales if your can of weedkiller is shown in the background. Presumably there must be some benefit, as there clearly must for a clothing manufacturer to have his label on jeans gyrating on the big screen. Exactly how much benefit there would be for you in such activities is for your commercial judgement; just don't get carried away because of the happy hours you spent in the back row of cinemas during your formative years. 'Product placement agencies' are springing up to help in the process and you may find the warmest welcome if hi-tech or high cost equipment or facilities are needed by a film maker.

At a more conventional level, you can sponsor a film or video in its own right or produce one to augment other sponsorship, such as a 'How to . . .' video on a sport you have helped or a 'Film of the Year' about a sponsored season.

If you embark on a video or film project, bear the following in mind:

- Get precise quotations from production companies before going ahead because budgets have a habit of being broken.
- Don't forget to budget for the cost of copies.
- Try to get videos into normal sales outlets, and put films into commercial libraries because it can be a nightmare handling loans of them in-house; if you use a reputable library they will monitor the quality of prints sent out for you. Loans can

either be free (with you paying library costs) or there can be a charge with you getting a portion of the receipts.
- Don't neglect in-flight outlets for your products – at least you will be fairly sure you are reaching the affluent.
- If you need various language editions of a film or video make this clear to the production people so that they avoid too many heads talking English to camera and allow enough footages for commentaries in languages which are wordier than English.
- Don't forget to show videos and films to employees.

Finally, if you are making a video of an event, you or your production company may be approached by amateur cameramen with footage (sportsmen can rarely make mistakes nowadays without someone capturing the moment); have a simple waiver form for them to complete giving you whatever rights you need to such footage (expect to pay a fee, of course).

Books

Sponsored books are yet another growth area and many publishers have special divisions to handle them.

You may ask why this book isn't sponsored. Well, it wasn't that I couldn't find a sponsor (it says here) but because I took a conscious decision not to do so as I wanted the book to be impartial (is there anything more ludicrous than an author standing on his dignity?). It illustrates one of the risks of sponsorship: if this book was sponsored by ASH or, conversely, the Tobacco Council would you believe I was totally honest in anything I wrote about tobacco sponsorship? I suspect not. (This scepticism extends to other areas too so that if a sponsored sport is a cliffhanger to the final minute of television coverage, there will be those suggesting a 'fix'.)

If you decide to get involved in book sponsorship, it need not be unduly expensive – guaranteeing a loss or committing to take a fixed number of copies may be enough to get you linked with a publication. You can use any copies you take as giveaways or make them self-liquidating. There is a view that a cover price gives a product more perceived value, but caution: if your sales people are busy, don't involve them in selling things like books – they may be missing more important leads while doing so.

What are the advantages of book sponsorship? These for instance:

- The subject matter and style can be tailored to fit your

promotional package.
- Books are an upmarket product and can be long-lasting (eg through library loans).
- You can aim books at your target audience fairly accurately.
- They can make good display material.
- There can be publicity for you via press reviews, author interviews and serialization or the publication of extracts. And there may be opportunities for exposure through TV tie-ins.

However, apart from launch parties, there may be fewer opportunities for client entertaining than with other more active forms of sponsorship, taking this area closer to sales promotion than pure sponsorship. Stamping your name on the front of a guidebook is of course simply sales promotion, just like having your own page in a diary mailed to clients, even though it may be called sponsorship. If you decide to go a stage further and genuinely sponsor an original work, do ask yourself one key question: *would the book stand up on its own without sponsorship*? If not, you may be straying close to vanity publishing, while the very act of publishing an unwanted history of your company may even make you appear a shade old-fashioned (especially if historic ads featured in it are sharper than your current ones). Such tomes are highly resistible and certainly don't count as art – which is why books weren't covered in the last chapter; personalized number plates for the commissioning executives cannot be far behind.

Conservation

Conservation is another growth area for sponsorship, not least because of the efforts of the World Wildlife Fund – UK. The Department of the Environment have agreed that the WWF will act as a central agency on behalf of the conservation organizations, and as a broker to handle enquiries from industry on wildlife and countryside conservation sponsorship. They hold a list of suitable projects (duly costed) and will be glad to give you a presentation if you are considering such sponsorship. It is an area towards which celebrities and, not least, TV are likely to be sympathetic and companies venturing into it may be pleasantly surprised at the professionalism of the people involved: the WWF approach stands comparison with that of any company, as does the literature produced by the Royal Society for the

Protection of Birds, whose brochure *Promotional Ideas for Eagle-eyed Marketing People* includes sponsorship as one of the suggestions. Other organizations produce good material too and I mention the RSPB simply because it is one of the most active, and the more active an organization is, the more likely it is to get support. Let us bush the good wine. Mind, it is probably easier to get sponsorship for beautiful things like birds than, say, snakes (although a 'save the adder' campaign might be suitable for an abacus manufacturer to sponsor).

Still on conservation, you could sponsor the restoration of a building (don't forget before and after photographs for any booklet you may produce) but if you are asked to sponsor an existing or new building (or a room in one), accept that, although you may build goodwill there is likely to be only one burst of publicity with little opportunity for ongoing stories.

Why not consider sponsoring archaeology? I must admit I would never have considered this had not Essex County Council (as a ratepayer I am one of their most committed sponsors) produced a booklet (sponsored of course) called *Your Company, Sponsorship and Archaeology* which does an excellent selling job. Worth sending £2 for a copy if you are interested in such sponsorship, or for that matter if you are seeking sponsorship and would like an example of a professional publication.

Charities

I am aware that many arts organizations have charitable status but here I am thinking of charities raising funds for the ill, disabled and so on. As pressure on funds grows, companies are increasingly going to be expected to do more for the community and, even if your shareholders don't entirely agree, there is surely nothing wrong with helping the fabric of our society. Charities are not always trying to get something for nothing but are becoming more professional in their approach to sponsorship, recognizing that they must give something in return for such funding. You may therefore find yourself approached for sponsorship by a charity in exactly the same way as by a sports body but with the advantage that there may be more overtones of good work and goodwill. Apart from special projects, you could sponsor a magazine for a charity, or a video about its work. The ways are manifold.

Miscellaneous

You don't always have to hand over money when sponsoring; for instance you can sponsor a 'loss' and simply guarantee the viability of an event. If you then work with the organizers to make it a success it may cost you nothing. Or you can offer your purchasing strength to get an organization its material (such as office equipment) at a discount. Of you can offer the use of your facilities, such as your factory car park as a gathering point for an event. Or you could second people to help an organization.

However, with any of these honourable methods it is sensible for both parties to try to put a rough value on what is being given and of course, what you will be getting in return. If you don't do this yet give substantial support (but not cash), the glory may go to a more 'formal' sponsor who has handed over a cheque.

To end this miscellaneous section let me briefly run through a few other things you could sponsor:

1. A local lecture, paying for the venue, posters, speaker's fee (if any) and so on.
2. A chair at a university in an appropriate area of interest to you. It should help to keep you in touch with advanced developments.
3. Prizes for a local event with 'Your Trophy' for this or that. (Don't forget to establish if the winner keeps the cup or gets a replica.) More general awards – such as for the most significant effort in an area – are usually a safe subject, particularly if you appoint independent judges to select the winners. (You can always blame them if the results are unpopular.) You can stretch your sponsorship mileage by following the progress of award winners.
4. A 'free' day or evening at, say, the theatre for a particular group you wish to reach who would otherwise have to pay.
5. Printed material to publicize an event. If you handle the printing you should at least be able to get your name spelt correctly.
6. A fun run or walk, perhaps with a local newspaper or radio as co-sponsor. The Department of Environment publish a leaflet 'Safety and Sponsored Walks' which should be required reading for such events.
7. Coaching for local youngsters.
8. Educational material such as wallcharts for schools (do not shade the information on them to suit your own ends).

9. Lollipop ladies or men. At least one headmaster has even tried to get sponsorship for a teacher.
10. If you are a lot braver than I am, you could sponsor a beauty contest but do work out in advance how you will maximize the press coverage if you attract the attention of feminists (you will).
11. Employees, by matching what they raise on a so-much-per-pound basis. But take care: if you support some in one fun run you may have to support more. Back to the importance of having a company policy.
12. An employee who is, say, a potential medal winner. Again, tread carefully so that you don't create jealousies.
13. A cabaret or table flowers or the printing of menus for a dinner organized by people you wish to reach.

Those are just a very few examples of what can be sponsored. And bear in mind that pure gimmick sponsorship may attract coverage, such as insuring *against* a ghost or monster appearing. If it is lighthearted enough the media will probably row along with you.

As I said at the beginning of the chapter, the sky really is the limit (or perhaps it isn't . . . who will be the first to sponsor an event on the moon?).

Chapter 9 **Drawing Up an Agreement**

If you have been subjected to a hard sell over a sponsorship project then, if time permits, try to pause for a final think before concluding negotiations. Is the deal really right for you and does it meet your objectives? If so, you are ready to negotiate. The process should end with something being *written down* because although a handshake may be fine among friends (although they may not remain so if the link goes sour), people move and change jobs, things get forgotten and disputes can arise; having things in writing will avoid a protracted 'he said, they said . . .' affair. A further advantage in drawing up a written agreement is that the process should hone your thinking on the fine details which can make or break sponsorship.

However, don't let talk of contracts get the relationship off on the wrong foot; stop short of a ruthless pound-of-flesh approach because the link will work best if people are cooperative and friendly. Even if you 'got away' with something because of a craftily drawn contract and a peculiarity in the law (and let's face it, it is peculiar) you would be unlikely to get the best out of those you sponsor and you could get a hostile press if you were seen to be too sharp. For this reason you should not try to build into a contract hopelessly unreasonable clauses or unachievable aims because they may simply lead to court. (I suppose it can't be long before a court case itself is sponsored.) To some extent your approach to negotiations may be governed by whether you are litigious by nature.

Get your legal boys to vet an agreement by all means but accept that if you have managed to coax a key sportsman or artist to consider joining you, and your legal eagles nitpick and poke for weeks over the small print, you may lose him – and it will serve you right. If you are dealing with amateurs with little business knowledge, take the trouble to explain any weird clauses you feel it necessary to build in and do make it all as clear as possible; too often the large print giveth and the small print taketh away. However, don't assume that amateur bodies will all be gentle and naive – some may be far more devious (and dishonourable) than professionals.

Two other general legal points:

1. Silence – by either negotiating party – does not necessarily mean acceptance; in fact it often heralds a breakdown in negotiations.
2. If there is no written contract and there is a dispute, then the courts will look at draft letters and consider verbal evidence. However, if there is a contract they will look at that and only that. So work towards at least a formal exchange of letters summarizing all you have agreed.

Who

All sound reasons for getting things sorted out properly at the start. And the first stage in the process is to be absolutely clear *who* is negotiating with you, what level of authority they have and if they can deliver what they promise.

Your own negotiating position should be equally clear and you need authority to act quickly in case it is necessary to pluck a prime plum (and they do grow from time to time even in such a buyer's market). You should get key decision-makers on board before proceeding too far with discussions. Unfortunately, the heady world of sponsorship seems to produce people who love all the wheeling and dealing but never actually commit to anything; don't add to the number. Avoid holding out false hope to people. This must be my third time of mentioning it but . . . do handle rejections with care to avoid antagonizing people.

Now a few general points on negotiating parties:

- If possible, negotiate with 'it', that is the activity itself, rather than through an agent. Certainly do so if a proposal has been presented to you by several agents. Also contact any national federation, association or whatever exists for the proposed activity if you are unsure.
- You may need more than one contract, for instance one for the activity and one for the promotional side.
- If you are dealing with a committee of an unincorporated association (such as a typical sports club), any clauses in a contract must accord with the association's constitution; if

you impose any which don't then they could be null and void.

- If you are dealing with one member of the committee of an unincorporated association, have the committee resolved that he can negotiate?
- If you are negotiating with someone under 18, they will need a parent or guardian to sign too.

What

Having sorted out who is negotiating, move on to establish *what* you are negotiating. If you have been promised various things then ensure that they are listed. You should consider all aspects of the link and note everything you can think of to avoid surprises later.

Some of the things you are likely to be negotiating are these:

1. The title of an event. The contract should stipulate that the sponsored activity must use the full title at all times and try to get others (such as the media) to do the same. You must be firm about this because if you once let the name slide, you will not get it back. Before signing a contract it is worth checking – in confidence – what the media's attitude to the whole thing is likely to be; better to discover in advance that they think the extra league or whatever you are proposing is totally unnecessary.

   Incidentally you will have more chance of the full name being used if it is a sensible one: 'The Harrison Challenge' will stand more chance than the 'The Harrison Eastern Counties Games, which may get abbreviated to 'The Eastern Counties'. Registering a name (not a complicated legal process) will put you on slightly firmer ground in getting it used.
2. The number of events covered by the agreement.
3. The territories covered by the sponsorship.
4. Decor. A vital area so be clear how an arena or 'thing' is to be decorated. If you want, say, a club to modify its colours to blend with your corporate ones or its members to wear hats with your logo for team photographs, spell this out in the contract.
5. The availability of participants for press interviews and other activities such as appearances in your factory or retail outlets. The number of days of their time you are entitled to should be stated.

6. Use of property to display. For instance, if you are sponsoring a powerboat, know how many days you can use it at trade shows.
7. Use of results in your advertising and promotional material without further payment.
8. The number of free tickets you are to receive for events.
9. If references over a public address are part of the package, the number should be stated.
10. If you are to be given product display areas at events, brief details should be listed so that you don't get pushed behind the bicycle sheds as the season progresses.
11. The use of your products where appropriate. If you are a soft drinks company sponsoring a sport you want participants to at least *appear* to drink your fluid; if they can't stand it they can always put another product in your cans (it happens).
12. Last, but by no means least, on this list: TV coverage. This is likely to be a key area although remember that many sponsorships work very well without TV. Establish who owns the TV and film rights to what you are planning to sponsor and, if there is any doubt over whether the activity will be televised, consider a two-stage deal of a basic sum with an additional payment dependent on coverage. There may be occasions when your weight as a sponsor will help to swing TV behind an activity because you will help to guarantee stability. Probe any TV agreements carefully because independent producers may make extravagant promises; be sure that they can deliver.

The list of things to be considered can be endless with major projects. Whatever the size, it is sensible to include a reference to the aims and objectives of the sponsorship, say 'to finish in the top half of a league' but only do so as a reminder, don't attempt to sue if the objective is not met.

I don't want to turn you into a suspicious old devil but do *check* what you are offered. Ask to see correspondence, in particular that involving the rights to this and that. A 'right' is simply a legal entitlement and you need to establish just who owns the rights to what you are sponsoring. Right? You may be able to acquire the rights to something direct from an association or governing body or they may appoint agents to act for them. Probe that they have *all* the rights you need; amateur organizations may not have too much control over their affairs so while they may have the rights to an event, check if that extends to the control of advertising at venues. And does their control extend to stipulating, say, that all participants must carry a particular name, namely yours?

Be cautious with 'packaged' events or where there are several sponsors; who will be the main sponsor and exactly what will you, as a secondary sponsor perhaps, receive? If you are the main sponsor, what control, if any, do you have over the others? Be cautious too with oddball events created just for TV or sponsors and, for example, establish if key stars will be allowed to compete. They will probably only be able to do so if the event is 'sanctioned' by the governing body; they may risk fines or bans otherwise.

Don't misunderstand me. I am not suggesting that you should expect things to keep crawling out of the woodwork. But I am suggesting that you should open your eyes before you open your cheque book.

Safeguards

Your caution should extend to building certain safeguards into a contract, such as:

1. Although a contract should stipulate the specific time for the sponsorship to operate, you should insist on an option to renew to protect your interest. If you back a new event and help to build it up, it is reasonable that you should have an option for further years; if you don't build something in then you may find your event marching off to other sponsors. Equally, of course, it is not unreasonable for an event to ask for an inflation clause so that their fee goes up; it is also reasonable that you should be asked to take up an option early enough to leave them time to find another sponsor if you don't renew. Incidentally, don't try to tie up potential superstars for too long – contracts can be broken and anyway it is pointless to try to force people to perform against their will.

2. If you suspect that the sponsored activity may not be able to deliver on a specific area, such as the display of banners, then consider building an appropriate clause into the contract. It is difficult, if not impossible, to assess what damage from loss of sales you are likely to suffer if a banner is not displayed, but it is better to try to agree a figure in advance than have squabbles on or immediately after the

day (a penalty clause may in fact serve to goad people into delivering what was intended).

3. If those you are sponsoring need to be given access to privileged information about your company, a confidentiality clause should be included. You may also care to include one stipulating that people should not criticize your company or its products in public. Care though: such clauses may attract adverse publicity if revealed. And by the way, before you rush to take out injunctions to stop this or that, keep in mind that the courts will be reluctant to grant them if paying damages would be a more suitable solution.

4. Set out things which either side should *not* do, such as accept clashing sponsorship or tamper with a beloved trademark or club badge. It may need to be made clear that those you are sponsoring do not acquire any rights to your trademark, nor do they become your agents or partners, nor can they pass on any rights to a third party without your agreement. If a special mascot or symbol has been created for an event, be sure you have the right to use it *before* placing bulk orders for paper hats or whatever featuring it.

5. How are any disputes to be settled? Anything, but anything, is better than resorting to the law; for a fairly informal local link you'd almost be better asking a local vicar or probation officer to act as a referee. Of course, both sides must be prepared to agree to accept such an arbitrator's decision otherwise you could still find yourself in the witness box. (I do not wish to be disrespectful to the Law, M'Lud, but it is difficult to take it too seriously when grown men don red dresses and wigs . . . and then admonish others for deviant sexual behaviour).

6. Include 'what happens if . . .?' clauses as appropriate to the link. What happens if a star falls ill? What happens if one of a series of events is cancelled? What happens if it rains? The more time you spend on contingency planning, the better the link will work.

7. If you have a specific interest in photographs of the sponsored activity, you may consider including a clause restricting other people's access for photography. However, you will be on weak ground because under English law there is no property in an image or likeness so you can't stop people taking photographs.

8. You may need cancellation clauses to let you escape if, say, a key performer gets involved in drugs or disorderly

behaviour. There may be other occasions when you need the right to terminate but this area will need careful negotiation; a difficulty may be that both negotiating parties will be aiming for the maximum length of time, for stability, but linked with the maximum amount of flexibility. Be practical: it is not sensible, for instance, to tie someone down for so long and so tightly that they go bankrupt.

Force majeure? Well, in these turbulent times I've reached the stage where I'm not sure about heaven or hell, and I'm beginning to have doubts about Milton Keynes, and certainly things could befall you which come into the unforeseeable category. If so, a contract will probably remain in force but you will not be able to get recompense for damage or delays caused. May the force not be with you.

Finance

Having sorted out what you are to get and built in suitable safeguards, all that remains is to establish what you are to pay in consideration of all the wonderful things that are to come to pass.

The person seeking your sponsorship should quote a price for the deal but this may well be a rough and ready figure. Invariably it will be linked to the person's needs, not to the market value of the package, because the majority of supplicants work out a budget then seek sponsorship to bridge any gaps; few do it the logical way which is to decide what the market will bear. As an extreme example; if a club needs £100 for a coffee machine they would be foolish to sell the rights to a televised sports meeting for that sum; equally if they needed £100,000 they would be unworldly to expect to raise it from an untelevised jumble sale.

The moral for a sponsor? Negotiate. Make an offer. If possible get a financial breakdown of what is on offer because, if nothing else, it may indicate if the organization is well run and if the people have done their sums properly. Have they prepared a cash flow forecast, for instance? You will be protecting yourself in checking the viability because an apparent bargain won't be one if the project collapses or has to be put on a financial life-support machine halfway through. Know who is to pay any licence or sanction fees and, if an agent is involved, who is to pay his commission (it will invariably be the person being sponsored).

Some organizations may give you access to their books but if so, don't expect elaborate company controls in, say, a small social club, and don't attempt to impose any either.

Decide if the sponsorship fee is to be index-linked for future years or if other calculations are to be used and, obviously, establish the method of payment – one-third in advance then equal monthly sums, or whatever. And do sort out your internal payment system; you may religiously take 90 days to pay suppliers but you should be slightly more flexible with sponsorship.

Having sorted out finance with the sponsored activity, budget internally too. Attempt to cover everything – temporary staff needed, mailing of press releases, stickers, giveaways, cost of erecting banners and product displays . . . you name it, include it. Budget for research to evaluate the success (or otherwise!) of the sponsorship then last, but certainly not least, add a hefty sum for contingencies.

Beware of ploughing money into 'general funds', because you may get a brief 'thank you' note and that's all, and whatever you sponsor, do try to allocate some funds to youth and/or to the general good of the activity; don't shovel it all to the stars.

If possible, hold a little back from your sponsorship spend so that you can either take advantage of additional opportunities which occur or perhaps make a gesture of goodwill after a success by, say, throwing a party which, by being unexpected, will help strengthen the link.

When budgeting you will of course remember to include a sum for promotion, won't you? How much? I wouldn't presume to tell you because there is no recommended percentage; some sponsors spend as much again on promotion, others more like 10 per cent. It depends on what you are sponsoring and how active you plan to be with back-up promotions and entertaining. And there is no marketing 'law' which states that you have to spend at the same level each year; there may be times when, in consultation with the sponsored activity, a heavy year could be followed by a light one before another major burst.

A few general financial considerations:

1. It may be wise to allocate the sponsorship sum as so much, perhaps one-third, for simply being involved (which will include the burst of launch publicity) and the rest spread on a per-event basis. This will make it easier to calculate reimbursements if events fail to happen.

2. If something belonging to one party has value added to it by another during the period of the sponsorship, establish beforehand who will benefit from the increased value. As an example, if you sponsor the restoration of an old boat and triple its value, who benefits?
3. If individuals are involved, who pays for their travel expenses, additional passes for their wives and so on? It may not matter who pays, it does matter that it is agreed in advance.
4. Who keeps any prize monies and trophies? Don't ask me – sort it out with whatever you are sponsoring.

Insurance

With all the variables in sponsorship, it makes sense to insure against whatever risks you can. You may, for instance, be able to get the sponsored activity to take out insurance to cover you if it all falls apart and they are unable to deliver what was promised. You should cover stunts and such things as cars as prizes for golfing holes in one, and you will be able to protect yourself against weather conditions and the non-appearance of a key person. In fact it is possible to insure against virtually anything, and don't forget that if you come up with a weird insurance proposal that in itself may get press coverage.

Tax

Although I've suggested you should not be over-hard nosed in dealing with people you are sponsoring, you should certainly have your accountant structure your affairs so that you (and the sponsored) benefit as much as possible from the tax rules. They are not especially clear.

Sponsorship is normally a tax-deductible expense when calculating business profits *if* it is of a revenue nature (ie not a capital payment – with one exception mentioned in a moment) and it is incurred wholly and exclusively for the purpose of trade. Repeat: for the purpose of trade. The Inland Revenue draw a sharp line between donations and sponsorship and if you want tax relief you've got to be acting to promote your product, services or name. So while sponsorship may be a legitimate business expense, patronage is not, although there are of course tax concessions for giving to organizations with charitable status. And if the activity you are sponsoring is a registered charity (as many arts organizations are, for instance) then it may be wise and more beneficial for them if you do so by covenant. In addition, companies are allowed to make one-off donations to registered charities, including the arts, of up to 3 per cent of their dividends with the recipient reclaiming tax paid; this is the exception I mentioned earlier because such payments can be made to projects of a capital nature.

Obviously you need to be crystal clear why you are sponsoring. If you are doing it to promote your products then that is a revenue expense and deductible; but if you do it to increase goodwill, that is patronage and not. For the same reason the purchase of a work of art by a company would be treated as a capital transaction, not sponsorship.

Entertainment expenses are not tax-deductible, although costs of employees and overseas customers are usually allowed. Entertainment should be incidental to and not the main purpose of the sponsorship if you plan to show the sponsorship fee as a deductible expense; this may mean care with an event where entertaining is the sole purpose. Then of course it may be that the VATman cometh too. It's never dull, is it?

If you want to pursue the subject further, the Association of Business Sponsorship of the Arts has published a book called *Business sponsorship of the arts – a tax guide*; one reason for publishing was as the basis of an ABSA campaign to increase the tax incentives available to businesses (it is easier in America for instance).

If you are giving to charity, the Inland Revenue's IR64 leaflet has a short section on sponsorship which includes the following:

> If you are in doubt about how a particular payment will be treated for tax purposes you should consult your Inspector of Taxes before making it.

Good advice. And here's some more: stay on the right side of the law. There may be a risk in sponsorship of back-handers or other 'inducements' and the line may be fine between bribes and gifts. Stay clean. And while you can by all means pay cheques to stars who have tax shelters in the Cayman Islands or wherever, I'd stop short of handing over suitcases full of cash.

Chapter 10 Making Sponsorship Work

You've ground through the legal side, you've handed over a cheque and posed for press pictures, so you can now forget about sponsorship and move on to other business affairs, right?

Wrong. Unless you *work* at sponsorship it will be less than 100 per cent successful and in fact a good project casually handled may get less coverage and be poorer value than a bad project which is well presented.

So: work hard. And now that the formal, legal side is out of the way, do appreciate that the link with the sponsored activity will work best if it is a *friendly* one. Above all, be committed, follow things through and keep your word; if you promise to do something, do it. Sponsorships can be a bit airy fairy at times so keep notes of what is said at meetings and confirm key points in writing afterwards, although do recognize that if it all falls apart, you can't force someone to do something, or even if you can you certainly can't make them perform at their best. Hence the need to keep things on a friendly basis so that those sponsored are anxious to give you value.

The person in charge of sponsorship in an organization should work to build a bridge to the sponsored activity, and the bridge should be a clear-cut and simple one avoiding too many layers of communication. If there are agents and managers all scrambling for their share of the decision-making it can become time-consuming and inefficient (and maybe even unpleasant). Even if there is a manager or agent involved as part of the interface, still try to build direct links to any stars involved in your sponsorship; if they get to know you they are more likely to consider or guard your interests.

You will need special care if you are one of several sponsors because if you don't watch your interests and insist on getting what you've 'bought', you may get shoved aside by more forceful partners. But here again, keep things on a friendly level if possible; to avoid strife it will pay to have a small steering group of representatives from the various parties meeting on a regular basis to coordinate activities. In fact such a steering committee can be beneficial for any sponsorship if it brings together sponsor's staff and the sponsored plus any sponsorship and advertising agencies involved in the link; your sponsorship executive should be the chairman. Incidentally, if your advertising agency were lukewarm about the sponsorship, do spell out the facts of business life to them so that they cooperate.

If you are sponsoring an event which is part of a championship then liaise with the overall championship sponsor, if any, as well as with sponsors of other qualifying rounds so that you coordinate press announcements and explore the possibility of joint efforts to extend media and public interest.

Keep employees informed and involved, not just because it is an obvious and nice thing to do but also because it may stave off criticism. If you sponsor a youth activity, older employees may think it is a waste of money (and vice versa of course) so keep them in touch with your aims and progress via notice-boards, newsletters, house magazines and so on. If appropriate, involve employees even further. Sponsoring a team? Get them along to meet staff and sign autographs. Sponsoring musicians? Ask them to give a concert on your premises or, better, take employees to a rehearsal where they can be given a chat on the background to your sponsorship.

Carry your link through to customers and trade promotions too. We will look at hospitality in the next chapter but if you are sponsoring something – like a car or boat – which makes an interesting static display then use it in showrooms, at exhibitions and so on. Involve the sponsored people too so that they get to understand a little about your world. Caution: moving displays and people around costs time and money, so who pays for what should be clarified at the start. If funds will stretch to it, a replica of the car, boat or whatever is desirable to avoid clashes when a display is needed during the vital days preparing for a major race.

To extend the sponsorship further, consider using trips to sponsored events as awards for sales contests for customers and your sales force, or for the general public via on-pack promotions or through newspaper competitions.

Plenty of opportunities? Of course there are, but (and there usually is one) do give whatever you've sponsored room to breathe. Don't, for example, book sportspeople for a sales dinner the night before they are due to take part in a key competition. Don't involve the sponsored people in so many requests for this, that and the other that most of their time is spent rushing around for you, with the result that they can't get on with their main task, whether it be winning things or whatever. If you push too hard you may get lack-lustre performances. Of course, if you don't promote at all you may be taken for granted; but strike a balance between being too laid back and too pushy.

Problems will be avoided if you plan as far ahead as possible and do such planning before, say, a sports or arts season starts because once it does you may simply get swept along by events without time for calm contemplation. Do a little 'crisis planning' too; consider what happens if it rains. What happens if a key star is injured? Or if the team doesn't win anything? Consider even more mundane things like how to get rid of litter after 5000 people have stood on a playing field to watch your sponsored fireworks display (if you don't plan what to do, you may get adverse press or public comment). If you are sponsoring a fairly involved and new event then, to remove some of the risk, consider running a small pilot event perhaps for employees; at least you may get a feel for how long specific things are likely to take.

After the pilot or, if you don't hold one, after your first actual event, hold an inquest with all concerned to consider how to improve things the next time. Don't forget to start by saying 'thank you' and even if a sponsored team loses its first game heavily, write a friendly note of encouragement – don't start whining. And don't forget the unpaid workers when saying thanks. Sooner or later a sport is going to run smack into the dichotomy of highly paid stars taking part in events which depend entirely on unpaid voluntary officials; as the stars and their managers grab for larger slices of the cake, can it be long before helpers suggest they should have at least a few crumbs? Perhaps not. To stave off the day in your particular field, consider a raffle with prizes for the helpers or throw a party for them at which they can meet the participants. Such things needn't be expensive but they will at least show the workers that they are not forgotten.

You may need to gently nudge people to work on your behalf to get you media attention, although if your team wins something, do discourage them from effusive praise for your help in a prize-giving speech. Although your aim may be to get your name mentioned, do realize that there is such a thing as overkill. If a young winner thanks his mum and dad for his success, everyone will smile indulgently; if he then goes on to gushingly thank you and list your 38 products people will just wince. On a larger scale, there was a horse race covered on national radio for which the sponsors had obviously helicoptered in celebrities and fed and watered them well. When the first VIP interviewed on radio plugged the sponsor (who shall be nameless) and the helicopter ride, it was fine. By the time the tenth had done the same it had become irritating to the ear and I suspect I was not the only one who vowed never to use the sponsor's products again. Don't indulge in the same overkill.

If your sponsorship is a success, consider widening its appeal by adding, say, extra categories the following year. If you wish to project individual brand names perhaps add the 'ABC Trophy' for this and that, and the 'XYZ Trophy' for that and this. But don't add so many divisions that you distract people from your main promotional thrust.

I am sure by now that you will appreciate that sponsorship is very different from many other areas of business life. There may (in fact almost certainly will) be more work involved but one of the joys of sponsorship is that there are also very many opportunities.

Advertising

Frequently, sponsorship has very direct links with other marketing efforts, not least advertising. For instance:

- The sponsorship package may include space in event programmes, perhaps with a rider preventing competitive advertising. I know the cost of setting ads can be high for such occasions but still try to tailor something for the particular target audience – they are likely to be aficionados who may not appreciate a repeat of a bland national ad.
- If the package includes free editorial space in programmes then give some thought to your words, don't sing your own praises too loudly or else you will sound off-key.
- If announcements about you over the public address are included in the deal, here again, choose the words with care. One of your best investments may be to offer to pay for a decent commentator, not so that he is in your pocket but because if people are kept properly informed and enter-

tained they will enjoy themselves that much more, and have a kinder view of you as a result. Incidentally, if you are involved in an obscure activity, do get the commentator to explain what is happening and, for instance, how the marking works (I've watched countless long jumps on TV but I've never heard a commentator explain whether the point counted is where the heels, buttocks or what land).

- On-air trailers for forthcoming events you are sponsoring may add to your coverage. Monitor that they actually happen if they are an agreed part of a deal.
- If appropriate, carry your sponsorship link across into your main advertising. I'm not suggesting you should run bold 'we won' ads the day after a success but if you are sponsoring a hi-tech activity perhaps include this in your ads as an indication of how you augment your R & D. But don't go overboard. Just as you should perhaps not use a national ad in a specialist programme, you should not confuse a national audience by running ads full of esoteric references to a minority activity you are sponsoring.

Advertising footnote: if you need to spend a huge amount on advertising in order to make the sponsorship come alive, maybe you are sponsoring the wrong thing and would be better just running an advertising campaign?

Decor

Another critical area. If you are to get full exposure for your money you must make sure that the sponsored 'thing', plus any support people and vehicles, are properly liveried. To get ideas, study what other sponsors do in the same field. Study other areas too; note, for instance, which logos on the cyclists on the Tour de France cycle race are most legible.

This area is so vital that it is desirable to draw up a guide (which may grow into a book) setting out exactly how things are to be decorated. Distribute the guide to everyone involved and do cover everything – if someone comes on with a bucket and shovel between horse displays, well, you may not want your logo on the bucket but you may feel that the bloke's overalls should be in a colour which blends with the general decor of the event.

Use your house colour(s) in your scheme of things to aid identification and incorporate your company logo where appropriate – the available space may not be large enough to carry your name, while on some occasions a logo may be more in keeping with the occasion. There are times when an over-brash display would be in bad taste and offputting; if you sponsor a school play, put a banner in the playground perhaps but not on the fairies' tutus.

Your guide book must cover all occasions and should stipulate what letters and sizes can be used for your company name, and when. The guide should cover clothing and vehicles too (and incidentally if you are linked with a sportsman, *listen* to his views on sports clothing). If the events you are sponsoring are part of a championship and the overall sponsor's decals have to be carried (on posters, etc.) then the guide should also make this clear.

All a bit nitpicking? It may seem so, but if you don't guard your interests and keep control of things, it will be entirely your fault if whatever you are sponsoring comes over on TV and in press pictures as a muddled mess.

Your guide should also set out what banners are to be displayed where and who is to put them up. If you are sponsoring one of a series of events, paying to display banners at other events in the series will help to extend awareness of what you are doing and will help make you an integral part of the particular activity.

If events are to be televised, there will be clear rules on how many banners you are allowed to display and when; work with, not against, TV companies when placing them. And remember that TV can distort slightly so experiment to get banners which are easily read; if your house style is a Shakespearean script, use a simpler typeface for banners because this is not an area for sophistication. Study the banners at the next televised sport you watch and you will see what I mean. A simple style will show up best in black and white newspaper photographs too.

Obviously, with the amount of detail it is likely to contain, your guide must be prepared before things get underway. It could include guidance on quite detailed things. For instance, if there is a start ramp and prize-giving area then spell out how these should be decorated. Even if there are only a handful of spectators they will still look better in photographs with a little 'style' – flags flying, trumpeters, balloons for children etc.

Incidentally, if elderly dignitories are to present awards don't make cups too heavy for them to hold and keep in mind that glass – while it makes nice trophies – can break. If a cup has a plinth, tie or tape it in place to prevent broken toes. Bear in mind that some people find winners spraying champagne offensive although the practice is well entrenched.

Have you ever wondered why laurel wreaths are going out of fashion for winners? Because they cover up logos on competitors' clothing. A ruthless old world, isn't it? But I guess you'd better join in, and if you want winners to wear hats with your name on as they collect their awards then have someone on hand to give them out. In fact you should have a 'bannerman' at events looking after all these areas; if you make a mineral water then he should be the one to see that the name on the bottle faces the cameras; he should be the one to guard against spectators draping coats on your carefully placed banners (incidentally, check where spectators in wheelchairs are placed before positioning your advertisements because hustling people out of the way would not be seen as a Good Thing).

The bannerman should also be the one to guard against competing teams swopping shirts after a match so that the losers' logo is the one photographed with the winners' cup (another example of how sponsorship can affect sporting traditions, not necessarily for the better).

Even after sterling efforts by the bannerman, you may still find sportsmen trying to be 'clever' over logos, covering them up or whatever, either because of competing contracts, bloody-mindedness or stupidity. In such cases take comfort from the fact that you do not have to renew the link the following year.

If all the dolly birds used to promote sponsorship links were laid end to end, no one would be unduly surprised but, if you have them at your events, do dress them in a style appropriate to the occasion – tight T-shirts and shorts for sports events perhaps, gowns for the arts (not just because of the culture clash but to avoid cardiac arrests among the men, who tend to be older than at sporting events).

Nearly finished, but there are just a few other areas which need attention:

- Incorporate your name and/or logo on all printed items – posters, tickets, programmes etc and do vet such material carefully to guard your interest. If you are linked with amateurs it may be wise to do the printing for them.
- Plan the range of printed items carefully – avoid a veritable cascade. However, don't try to straddle too many audiences with the same material – what suits key customers may not be appropriate for schools (for which a project pack with posters and so on may be more worthwhile).
- Stickers are always popular; obviously they should reflect the overall theme of your printed material.

- If you design a range of clothing and posters for the sponsored activity, consider selling the material. Mind, take care not to waste too much time on it – executives who take seconds to make major investment decisions may argue for hours over the design of a T-shirt. It will probably make sense to use an outside agency to handle clothing, and don't expect to make a large profit, just be glad of the extra visibility which will result. If you sponsor a winter sport I suppose you could even build your logo into the soles of shoes to show in the snow.
- Don't forget youngsters. Can models of whatever you sponsor be made in your colours? If so, they will also make nice mementoes for customers you entertain at events. In fact, if you commission a small limited edition of a vehicle, say a horse transporter or van in your colours, they might even appreciate in value as collectors' items.
- If a model wouldn't be appropriate, would a jigsaw featuring a photograph of the activity work instead?
- Can a computer game be developed based on the sponsored activity?
- If you sponsor something which has a body of fans, prepare appropriate material, postcards of the stars and so on, for them. And if the link involves a fan club, see that it is properly run and gives value for money; not all of them do.
- Consider using clothing, jigsaws and so on as raffle prizes for employees and customer occasions, as well as for local charity events.

Let me stress that the ideas in this chapter are by no means exhaustive – there may be many other things you can do to promote your particular sponsorship. I know I may have made it all sound like hard work, but you must pay attention to detail and work at sponsorship to get value for your money.

Chapter 11 **Entertaining**

Entertaining clients is one of the main reasons for sponsorship, and rightly so, because if customers or others you seek to influence are your guests, they are a captive audience, and if a sponsored event is organized properly it can be an excellent way to mix business and pleasure. But because your company, as well as the event itself, will be 'on show' you must ensure that the planning is perfect.

Invitations

The planning should extend to taking great care with your invitation list because the anger of people inadvertently left off it may undo the good you do with those invited. To avoid ruffled feathers, your in-house invitation list needs care too but I suggest that you avoid guests being hopelessly outnumbered by company people – simply giving yourself and your colleagues a jolly day out shouldn't really be the object of the exercise, should it?

When planning, you will need to decide whether to invite children; there may be less chance to do business if you do (not that it is likely to be an occasion for a hard sell anyway) but you will be better regarded if children are included and the atmosphere may be more relaxed and friendly. Decide too if any local dignataries, politicians and the like should be invited; you will find that, apart from a very few puritans, they will march to the trough as willingly as anyone else. If any politicians are known to be enthusiasts for what you sponsor then consider inviting them even if they are not your local MPs – you never know when you may need friends.

Add some style to your invitation; personalize it, make it friendly and consider building up interest in the run-up to the date by, for instance, posting programmes to invitees. If you are sponsoring a fairly esoteric activity, consider a guidebook or pamphlet explaining it all to the layman and mail it to your guests a few days in advance. Incidentally, if your function clashes with a major event, such as a Wimbledon final, have TV available and mention this in your invitation. As an aside, you may need to consider how important the size of the actual audience is at your event. It may not matter, although serried ranks of empty seats at a sport hardly make it look a success, particularly if the gaps appear on TV. If there is unlikely to be a full house, perhaps explain why to your guests so that they do not consider you have backed a loser.

Invitations should guide people on dress and if weatherproof clothing is likely to be needed, arrange to have an emergency supply available plus umbrellas.

Monitor the response to your invitations while there is still time to send out more if it seems you will be light on numbers.

Work out a careful timetable for the occasion which strikes a balance between rushing people around and being so leisurely over lunch that guests miss the main action. Overall planning is one area where you may be glad of outside help from people who know, for example, how long it will take 100 people to settle in a marquee and scoff your salmon salad.

Travel

Movements in and out can be time-consuming and harassing at some major sporting events so, again, plan carefully, bearing in mind that not everyone is wild about helicopters to leapfrog traffic queues. If guests are arriving by car, try to fix a special area for them to park near the action, while if you move people by coach advise them if coats and packages can be left on board during the day; at open-air events a coach may make a useful base – if there are car parks full of them, put a clear identifying sign on yours.

However people arrive at a function, they must have the right tickets or passes and if, for instance, you have your own hospitality area you must brief any commissionaires properly and also have someone with tact near the door who knows your guests; if you don't you can be sure the one person turned away will be a key customer. Incidentally, having the 'right passes' does not necessarily mean that your guests should be given access to areas where they will be a nuisance and get in the way of the main action. Again it is a question of balance; if you want customers to see behind the scenes of what you sponsor, why not arrange visits to training sessions or rehearsals? These can be built up into very exclusive occasions (if anyone can gain access to something then maybe it hasn't got enough style). Private views of art exhibitions will go down well, as may a function at a stately home which is normally closed to the public (his lordship will probably put in an appearance too if the money is right). And don't neglect the impact of your customers rubbing shoulders with celebrities on the golf course.

A pre-briefing session should be held with company attendees to establish who will be looking after whom; there should be one or two free floaters to keep an eye on things in general. Make guests feel welcome and that they are attending something rather special; involve any celebrities in the process (people do like to meet them) although don't expect someone to do party tricks just before they run, play, sing or whatever.

Product demonstrations? They are unlikely to be appropriate although a display of your wares may be. Speeches? They too will depend on the occasion but if, say, someone makes a brief speech of welcome or introduces a star, then do liaise with the caterers to avoid the noise of plates being stacked and so on; noise can be a particular problem in marquees but sponsored events are unlikely to be the setting for long speeches anyway. Incidentally, if you've had a special hospitality unit made, do extend its use, for instance at town shows, employee open days and the like.

Refreshments

At many events you may have to use the on-site caterers. If so, be clear exactly what you are buying and do get things in writing. And when budgeting for food and drink, allow a contingency sum because the chief executive may want to break open the champagne if a team wins or a soprano manages to hit all the right notes. By the way, if you are a co- or subsidiary sponsor, you may ease your workload and budget by 'buying in' to arrangements being made by a major sponsor – if someone is inviting 100 people he may be prepared to quote to tag on your 10 or so customers.

Caterers will almost certainly have set menus at various prices. Tailor what you order to your guests and, to some extent, to the event itself: strawberries and cream may be mandatory at Wimbledon but might get you strange looks at a motorcycle scramble in November. If in doubt, stick to fairly conventional food unless of course you have sponsored a chef in which case you could run wild with special evenings – even run an Egyptian one and get him to serve the sauce of the Nile.

When catering, serve as high a standard as you can afford and extend the principle to apparently mundane things too – if you only serve coffee and biscuits then make them good quality; it is foolish to spend on sponsorship and then cheesepare and serve ale when champagne would be more appropriate (although consider having ale and fruit juices available too). You presumably know your own guests but bear in mind that, while I am sure they are charming people, drink, heat and excitement (and maybe betting) can occasionally lead to unruly behaviour. Just be gently on your guard and perhaps slow up the refill rate for likely troublemakers. If there is a known drunk who you simply have to invite (although I can't think why) then delegate a 'minder' to look after him. More drinks will be consumed if you are paying, as they will if waitresses circulate with trays to save people having to go to a bar. It is up to you to set the style. Don't be so stingy that someone gets up and proposes a toast to 'absent friends, coupled with the name of the wine waiter' but, equally, don't slosh the drinks about so much that your guests feel it is just a boozing session. Your side shouldn't drink too much of course.

Finally, after the ball is over, follow up by, say, sending a souvenir photograph or two to everyone who attended, together with a 'thank you for coming' letter. Tongue-in-cheek certificates stating that guests took part in some heroic deed may be popular and if they are framed by recipients (as is likely) will make the memory linger on.

Don't neglect other opportunities to 'entertain' people, for example get sponsored stars to give talks or take films to local groups, not forgetting your own employees. And if you hear of people giving regular talks on sponsorship (this is becoming a growth industry), why not feed them with information and illustrations of what you do? If they use you as an example it will help to spread the word that yours is a lively company.

Chapter 12 The Media

When it becomes clear that your negotiations to sponsor something are likely to prove fruitful, stress to the sponsored people that they should not rush from a meeting and tell the world that Santa Claus has come to town. You need a more considered approach if the announcement is to get attention. The launch is likely to attract the greatest single burst of coverage your sponsorship receives although the amount may depend on the country; in some, sponsorship is itself regarded as news, in others the media may go out of their way to avoid mentioning a sponsor – a golf tournament important enough to attract 30,000 spectators in Paris was described on TV as being 'sponsored by a major manufacturer'.

If you are announcing a significant sponsorship then hold a press conference to do so but don't waste journalists' time if it is a tiny low-key project, send them a press release instead.

If you are new to sponsorship *and* public relations (where have you been all these years?), you should consider getting professional advice, for instance over the choice of venue. Hold the press conference at whatever you are sponsoring if appropriate, as it will be with a theatre or sports facility, but don't expect a massive turnout if you try to drag journalists too far. When selecting a venue it is worth finding one with a separate room which can be used for radio and TV interviews.

What level of hospitality you decide to lay on for journalists will be up to you but don't expect a venue to cater above its class if you are serving a meal. If you ply journalists with drink they may be less critical if the conference goes awry; coffee before and drinks after the conference is perhaps the best plan.

Cast your net wide when drawing up the invitation list for a press conference. Invite local journalists plus ones from the technical press (if any) covering your industry plus correspondents covering the activity you have decided to sponsor. Invite the key people involved in whatever you are sponsoring, in particular any stars to whom the press will wish to talk. If an important person is away at the time then consider getting them to phone the conference venue at a specific time so that they can be questioned on a squawk box; the fact that you have made such an arrangement will show journalists that you are serious about the sponsorship. People phoning in should assume everything they say is being overheard – they should not mutter that 'it's a total shambles' as they are first put through.

Give careful thought to what should be said at the conference and who should say it. There may be merit in the people being sponsored making the announcement; their outline of your charms will sound less boastful than if it comes from you, although you can help them write the words of course. Whoever speaks should not grind on too long, nor should anyone imply that he 'expects' media mentions.

Have press releases available spelling out your news, and if you plan special printed material for the sponsorship your press release paper should reflect the same style. Don't agonize too long over the words in a press release, you are not writing a Great Novel, but do answer the 'Ws': who, what, when, where and why. Releases should be typed, with wide margins and double spacing, on one side only of A4 paper. Get to the point quickly because if a story is too long journalists are likely to cut the last paragraph or two (or three). Include the phone number of a contact in case more information is needed. Be cautious in trying to impose an embargo on sponsorship news because journalists may well consider the information not important enough to warrant one and will choose to ignore it.

So that both sides speak with one voice (ie tell the same tale) it is worth drawing up a question-and-answer sheet (a 'Q and A') which lists all the questions you are likely to be asked, however nasty, with suggested answers. Ask people not to leave such sheets lying around as they may alert journalists to awkward issues which they would not otherwise have considered. Don't let the preparation of a Q and A make you assume that journalists will necessarily be hostile in their questioning; just be prepared. Your answer to 'Why are you sponsoring a ballet when you've just announced major redundancies?' will flow better if you've considered it in advance. (Why are you, by the way?) If you are sure you will get hard or hostile questions on an issue then get a 'tame' journalist to ask them early on or have an apparently hard-hitting interviewer quiz you; either way may give you a gentler ride than leaving things to be raised spontaneously.

One area you can safely assume people will probe: the amount of money involved in the sponsorship deal. You can build a confidential clause into a contract if you wish, and you are not compelled to reveal figures of course, but as most sponsorship sums *are* announced you may be considered unduly coy if you don't tell all.

Take care to get any product link and sponsorship philosophy over at the launch conference and if you have prepared special posters, banners or whatever then have them on display. Explain to any trade press exactly what you are up to and why (they will be important to you long after the sponsorship has ended), and then involve them because even a dry old technical journalist may enjoy a day out of the office visiting your sponsored activity.

Three other points on press conferences:

1. Don't overdo product plugs to hardbitten journalists nor make them feel that they are simply being treated as a link in your marketing chain (even if they are).
2. Don't make hostages to fortune by boldly claiming that 'your' team is going to win this or that.
3. Take care to send press material to journalists who couldn't attend the conference.

Television

Get off your knees – TV isn't as great a god as some of those working in it may think. In fact you should be careful that you don't genuflect to TV so much at your launch conference that press people get annoyed. My guess is that as the clutter grows, TV coverage of sponsored activities may get less important; hospitality and building goodwill will be much more significant.

But despite my caution, TV is still important and do recognize that satellite TV means virtually no frontiers, and programmes featuring your sponsorship may appear around the world. Get to know the key people involved in programmes covering whatever you have sponsored to see if they need, or will use, video clips supplied by you of training sessions or whatever. These may be made as part of an ongoing record of your sponsorship which could result in a 'video of the year' to loan or sell to enthusiasts.

Work too to improve the quality of TV coverage by, for instance, cooperating to put cameras in new or unusual places (note how common they've become on racing cars for instance). Anything which excites viewers will increase their numbers and will help the sponsored activity and, of course, the sponsors involved. If the viewing figures are raised by your efforts, the TV companies will be that much keener to continue the coverage in future seasons.

Monitor such things as mentions of your name in TV programme guides. Not important? Well, I agree that a reference is hardly going to send people rushing out to buy your goods, but if you once start to let such details slide, you will be on your way to becoming a slipshod sponsor.

Radio

Don't ignore radio; its need for material is as insatiable as television's. Obviously you should invite local radio stations to send people to your launch conference or offer to call in to discuss things live. Establish what their policy is towards syndicated tapes; many people mail these to radio stations on a regular basis with just a sentence (or two) of a corporate message, for example a building society may send out an interview on interest rates and be happy with just one or two mentions of its name. Although some stations have a policy of not using such material, can you produce such tapes, say, before and/or after each event you sponsor for those that do? If you build up a system like this don't overdo the plugs for your company or the material will definitely not be used. If you advance to sponsorship of major events you may need to consider setting up a special radio network to feed out material.

Photographs

In all the crackle and pop of radio and television, don't neglect the snap of simple black and white photographs. Don't let any appear without showing proper livery; if you are sponsoring a team of horses then decorate the transporter *before* any team photographs are taken (it need only be done on one side with stick-on material rather than paint if time is short). If you neglect this, the first photographs released may be the ones which get put on file and used . . . and used, all the while without your logo.

Other points on photography:

- Have colour as well as black and white photographs available, and remember that they should all be carefully captioned. Prints should be at least six inches by eight.

- Supply artwork and colour references of any logos, symbols, event names, maps and so on which you hope to get used.
- Keep a library of photographs to refer back to if, for instance, a young unknown you sponsor today becomes a big name tomorrow.
- If you have something or someone who will make news and you have a lot of guests at a function, photograph them with the attraction one after another on an assembly line basis. Put a reference number in a discreet corner of each picture and log the number on, say, people's visiting cards to aid identification, then – with their permission – send the photographs to appropriate local papers; if guests are photographed with a celebrity, the press usage may be surprisingly extensive.
- If you hand over a blown-up cheque to inaugurate a link, have one specially prepared with your name in bold type otherwise all you will be promoting may be the bank.
- Consider photographic competitions based on whatever you are sponsoring. Camera clubs training lenses on your logo won't be any hardship and a few items of team clothing may suffice as prizes.

One final point on photography: be wary of trying to prohibit people from taking photographs. It is possible to do so in theatres for copyright reasons but it could make you unpopular at other events.

Ongoing press liaison

Once the first flush of enthusiasm is over, you will have to work continuously to maintain media interest in your sponsorship. Your efforts should be dovetailed with your normal day-to-day PR efforts – it would be foolish to call journalists to a sponsorship press conference within a day or so of one on a new factory extension.

As good communications are vital for sponsorship to work, it is worthwhile issuing a regular newsletter either monthly, or before or after every event. It should go to all the participants as well as employees and press. In addition to this regular information service, stories should be fed to the press on an *ad hoc* basis; sponsorship may offer oddball opportunities for stories and photographs which will help to show you in a friendly light.

In all your dealings with the media, remember that most of them are under extreme commercial pressures. Newspapers are not in business simply to plug sponsors and they are not compelled to mention you or your products. However, the media need sport, sport needs sponsors, sponsors need the media, so it only needs the media to give sponsors reasonable coverage for the circle to be completed. *But* let me repeat: newspapers are not compelled to mention you so don't indulge in bullyboy tactics if you feel you are getting inadequate coverage. It has been known for journalists to be shunned by sponsors for not giving them enough coverage; such crass behaviour shows a singular lack of awareness of PR among other things. It may be far better to ask the people you have sponsored to see if they can coax papers into being more responsive.

If the activity you are sponsoring has few skills at dealing with the press then offer to help. The more alert national associations (for sport, for instance) are, or should be, laying down 'cat sat on the mat' press guidelines for clubs under their wings; if they aren't then you should help your particular activity to function efficiently. Your guidelines should advise, for example, that before an event journalists should be sent:

- Press releases about the event, together with pass(es) as appropriate.
- Copies of any programmes and other background material, such as the regulations in the case of a sporting event.
- Details of the press office: location, opening times, etc.
- Name of the press officer and phone numbers. (As the sponsor you should consider having at least one of your people at every event to look after the press.)
- Lists of local accommodation when necessary.
- Details of any special arrangements for photographers.

If a journalist is added to the list at a late stage, remember to send him releases already issued to bring him up to date. If budgets will permit, putting material into a press 'pack' will add a little style, as will clipboards and the like as souvenirs for journalists.

Your guidelines should also suggest what arrangements are needed for an efficient press office: how many telephones, seats, desks, telexes, typewriters, boards on which to pin press releases, pigeon-holes for journalists through which to distribute releases and so on. Plus a bar, of course. If a press conference is to be held, perhaps for interviews with winners, then the guide should mention the need for a microphone and stress that a clear space should be kept in front of winners' podiums for photo-graphs. All obvious? Maybe to you but not necessarily to a small association, so help it. Incidentally, if you draw up a press manual, do make it user friendly; don't fill it with jargon or be too dictatorial. Obviously the degree of detail needed will depend on the scale of the event; for many the idea of telexes or a photo-developing service would be absurd, for others a mobile press room travelling around could be essential.

Don't let the hardware blind you to what journalists want most of all: news of what is going on, so work to develop a quick information service and also establish quite clearly who is to be the spokesman if something goes wrong; if there is a squabble over results it is important that one – and only one – person is issuing statements *and* doing it quickly enough so that you are not wrongfooted by 'the other side' whether it be the organizers or a competitor.

More things are likely to go wrong if you have big stars involved (although your coverage should be greater because the media interest will be higher and some may already have press contacts or even contracts (which will need careful handling). If a star has been involved in a scandal then the press will major on that rather than on what you've sponsored, but you didn't sponsor stars expecting them to be faceless and grey, did you? Even if a star plays silly devils and deliberately doesn't use your product there may still be a friendly diary piece in it for you. I can't stress enough that sponsorship is not as straightforward as advertising or printing 'tuppence off' on a can. It is more complicated than that but it also offers far more opportunities.

Just a few brief final points on the media:

- If whatever you sponsor wins something, expect calls from advertising representatives asking you to advertise your success. Keep your head.
- Look for oddball opportunities. If an individual you sponsor builds model boats as a hobby ask him to decorate one in your livery and send out photographs (include the hobby magazines of course).
- Bookmakers may well quote odds on what you sponsor, however bizarre, with opportunities for a press story.
- Although stunts may have their place in your media planning, don't let them get out of hand. Journalists will resent being too obviously manipulated and, worse, the rescue services (and public) will not be impressed if people

have to be saved from danger because of something you dreamed up.

- Note the growth of spot-the-difference competitions in newspapers, often with trade names featured. Perhaps you can issue artwork for a contest featuring what you sponsor with, say, team clothing as prizes.
- If you make a film or video about your activity, enter it for awards. The industry loves to congratulate itself and there are plenty of prizes around; if you win a category you will have a peg for a brief press release.
- Don't be over-modest if, as a result of what you sponsor, money is handed over to a charity – the recipients may find that publicity for your act nudges a few consciences.
- Keep in mind that you may be able to get media coverage by simply letting word get around that you are *thinking* of sponsoring something without going on to actually do so. Rather a cynical and dangerous practice. But it happens.

Chapter 13 Problem Areas

It is perhaps appropriate that this chapter should be unlucky thirteen because not all sponsorship links run smoothly and there can be problems; many of these could be avoided by careful planning but in the eagerness to get on with things this important step may be neglected.

It is essential not to abandon your normal business sense when sponsoring. Don't get excited or fall in love with an activity or with the stars. And stay objective because, if you don't, you may find the sponsorship is taking up a disproportionate amount of the company's time; don't be sidetracked from your main business aims.

Honeymoons can be short in sponsorship and press interest will drop, initial enthusiasm will fade, promised stars may not be available and you, the sponsor, may be taken for granted (particularly if your cheque has removed the financial millstone hanging over an activity). Too often the major effort is put into *selling* a sponsorship link and not *servicing* it, with the result that sponsors are disappointed with what they get; this may apply particularly to new activities where all concerned are learning together. But if your sponsorship doesn't generate the interest you were expecting, *it is probably your fault*. Crack the whip and work at the link. If you just start whingeing about things not working you will simply be seen as a moaner.

Keep in mind that not everyone may be enthusiastic. Some of your customers (and shareholders) may be lukewarm and will need 'selling' on the benefits, otherwise they may feel you have curious business methods. Even inside the company there may be hostility; people who will rarely criticize an ad may be more willing to attack sponsorship. Your activities may even attract criticism from a wider public if, for instance, you put up incongruous banners at events (the planning people may have a view about these too of course).

As the sponsorship progresses, keep evaluating the

commercial benefits. If sports stars' fees escalate (and, it must be said, some sports become ludicrously self-important) and the general sponsorship clutter increases, you may even decide that more conventional marketing methods will be more cost-effective in future. Sponsorship is not a merry-go-round that you *have* to ride.

On a broader front, the political risks with sponsorship have already been mentioned but there are other concerns. Sponsorship can, and often does, erode sporting standards; it can increase the pressure to win (both glory and money) and it can lead to cheating and to barrack-room lawyers studying the small print of sporting regulations to an unhealthy degree. Winning can perhaps become too important; try not to let your sponsorship introduce such distortion.

And sponsorship can actually detract from competitive performances if, for instance, participants have to interrupt training to pose at photocalls, meet customers, and so on. Sponsorship can also have an adverse effect if the money unbalances a club so that it stops trying to be self-sufficient in other ways.

Vow not to despoil anything you sponsor. If the activity ends up taking second place to your sponsorship, your efforts may actually be working to turn people off you. The risks of starting a motor race in marginal safety conditions to suit TV should be obvious (if they aren't, then maybe you aren't safe to be a sponsor) but even less dramatic changes may have an adverse knock-on effect; for example, before shortening an event for TV consider if this could lead to an increase in drug taking by participants because of a changed play pattern. Extreme? Perhaps, and I'm *not* suggesting that you should stay in a time warp with no change at all; just be a shade cautious.

Don't try to take over and run what you are sponsoring. The erosion can be slow but steady. Delay the start time to suit your client entertaining? Certainly, sir. Finish a shade early so that a helicopter can land on the pitch to take guests away? Of course. Change the white ball to red because it's the favourite colour of the chairman's wife? Well . . . I hope you see the dangers. And keep in mind that every exhibition game will tend to devalue the mainstream events in whatever you are sponsoring.

There are concerns about other areas of sponsorship too, such as sponsored (whether officially or unofficially) radio or television programmes with, for instance, a travelogue accepting free tickets in return for the mention of an airline. Harmless? Maybe, but how objective is the programme likely to be towards viewers' complaints about that particular airline?

I don't want to reduce you to despair because most sponsorship links work happily, just be on your guard against problems. Such as these, for instance:

- Consider an activity's regular supporters as well as your VIP guests. You will create ill-will if the former can't get a ticket or, if they do, fail to see all the action because of special arrangements you have made for your customers.
- If people are offended by something you have sponsored, they may complain to and about you, however little say in things you may have had.
- Watch that your actions don't give PR opportunities to your business rivals; if, for instance, you ban a banner at a ground that has been there since day one, you may get slated for strongarm tactics.
- Any behind-the-scenes 'deals' with TV companies may make sleazy reading if they get exposed in the press.
- A mild but inevitable problem: if you sponsor one thing you will be approached by many others, which is why you need one person handling all the letters so that you have a consistent response.
- The area you sponsor may need a cash injection halfway through the programme, and you may get moral blackmail that it would be bad for everything to stop. If you do decide to help out on such occasions at least get something in return and, before handing over more money, insist on seeing the books and the plans because you may just be postponing an inevitable collapse.

A fairly delicate sponsorship problem may be knowing when to *stop*. Sponsorship tends to have a natural life and it is better to stop before people get bored with what you are doing, but do phase out elegantly and give plenty of warning to avoid cries of people being left in the lurch.

Really, all this chapter emphasizes is that you simply have to be involved and aware. Take the media for example: the sheer hype for an activity can slip out of your control and if the public get satiated it may be a devil of a job to rekindle their interest (think how you instinctively switch off the TV the moment someone appears with whom you have become bored). Being alert should also keep you in tune with trends as well as events in the wider world which could affect your sponsorship – being linked with a motorized sport could be a negative in an energy crisis, for instance.

Not surprisingly perhaps, many sponsorship problems are to do with *people*. For instance:

- An intermediary, such as a PR company or sponsorship agency interfacing between you and what you sponsor may cause friction. If so, try to forge direct links.
- People may move on either side. Just as a new broom on the company side may want to change things, so the departure of a key person on the sponsored side may produce a change in attitude.
- Some sponsored activities and their agents – and, conversely, some sponsors and *their* agents – may try to get more than their fair share from a deal. Sponsorship is increasing so fast that inevitably it has attracted a few fast-buck merchants with no long-term interest.
- A sponsor may face unruly behaviour by a star through drink, drugs or whatever. If you are an established company, take stock: do you really need such hassle? Don't believe the tale that any publicity is good publicity. It isn't, so consider cutting your losses.
- Expect there to be problems between old timers running sports and temperamental stars (temperamental has been defined as 50 per cent temper and 50 per cent mental, which is not far wrong in some cases). Careful you don't get caught in the crossfire. Should there be a court case it is likely to be long and juicy but it may not help your reputation or sales curve.

Finally, beware of clashes between sponsors of individuals, teams, events, championships and maybe even national organizations. Clashes may be inevitable where, for instance, a participant with sponsorship from one fizzy drinks company takes part in an event sponsored by a rival brand, which qualifies for a championship supported by a third make, and it all takes place at a ground carrying the banners of a fourth. No one said it would be easy. But if logos have to be taped over and banners blocked out it can all appear pretty petty.

Chapter 14 Analysing Results

Relatively few sponsors evaulate their efforts with any degree of sophistication; most rely on a general feel for such things as media coverage and feedback from employees and customers. Research is poor partly because it is difficult to know just what to measure; you can check how many people read a particular ad but sponsorship has more variables such as the media coverage, the excitement, the good will and so on. If sponsorship is fully integrated into your affairs – as it should be – it may be difficult to measure which action contributed what to a shift in reputation.

From time to time, general market research on sponsorship appears which purports to be terribly meaningful but, as with so much research, have the salt cellar handy when you read it; what is claimed to be an elaborately structured survey may in fact be the result of questionnaires which were completed by office juniors (I know it happens). Even the time market research is done will have an affect on results – a sponsor will obviously rate higher in research carried out shortly after his sponsored event has been televised.

Some businessmen maintain that they sponsor 'until they reach their target', but if they don't evaluate, how do they know if they have done so? Mind, research may be so casual because the results may not always be what is desired; ignorance throughout a company may be bliss for the sponsorship executive concerned.

Despite this, you should beware of a warm corporate glow as your only reward; you should at least try to track if sponsorship is working for you; the degree of effort may well depend on the level of expenditure on sponsorship, of course. One thing is certain: you can only attempt to measure the results of sponsorship if your objectives were clear at the start, so take out the ones you set all those chapters ago and try to assess if you are meeting them. And let me repeat an earlier point: an objective must be one the sponsorship is capable of meeting. Don't set unrealistic targets and, to be fair to the sponsorship, try to assess what would have happened if you *hadn't* sponsored. Just holding sales in a plummeting market could be a triumph.

If you do regular studies on your company image through properly structured market research, you should be able to detect if sponsorship is working, but with either existing or newly commissioned research, be careful to differentiate between *awareness* and *attitude*. Sponsorship which gets substantial media coverage should certainly increase people's awareness of you, but you also need to know what their attitude to you is. This will be influenced by what you sponsor, which is why the point has been stressed that you should match this carefully to your requirements. If you sponsor a local football team, the town may well be *aware* of it, but householders who have to contend with hooligans may take the *attitude* that you as the sponsor are an equal hooligan for encouraging the activity; perhaps not the image you were seeking.

Obviously, if at all possible you should conduct research *before* you commence sponsorship (so that you have a benchmark) and then *during* it while there is still time to change direction if necessary – with the caution that you will rarely see dramatic or immediate shifts in awareness (or leaps in sales for that matter).

But how should you measure the effects of sponsorship if you have neither the funds nor inclination for scientific market research? Well, Sportscan offer a monitoring service for sports sponsors of TV and press coverage and provide figures showing, for instance, just how much airtime an activity receives. Or, for any form of sponsorship, you may care to measure your own press coverage from clippings and sit some poor devil in front of a TV set with a counter and stopwatch to log name mentions and the length of time your banners appear; you could keep a similar count for radio mentions. But all these methods need considerable caution. The activity you sponsor got 57 minutes of TV coverage? Tremendous. Your banners appeared on screen for 14 minutes? What joy. But on no account try to equate that 14 minutes with the same amount of paid-for airtime because, while you or your record keeper may have noticed your banners for that long (well, you would, wouldn't you?) is it likely that the general public will have studied them so avidly? Of course not; they will have been watching the main action instead.

The same realism is needed over press references. If you clip something out of a newspaper and photocopy it for wider circulation, say to senior management, do realize that your very act of taking the item out of context has distorted its importance. If you then circle your logo in press photographs or colour-highlight references to your name in the text (and, amazingly, people do have the time and money to waste on such things), you have simply added to the distortion. The result may be to give a spurious importance to something hardly noticed, or long forgotten, by a wider public.

Of course, as a crude measure it is better for your banner to be in vision for 14 minutes than 10, which is why being near, say, scoreboards where the TV cameras tend to linger may be better than more frenzied places. But just accept that any such measurements are, at best, a crude guide – you will still need to use your judgement in evaluating the affects of sponsorship.

There may be other indicators to guide you: if you become a friendly butt for cartoonists, you will have succeeded, as you will if your sales representatives find doors half open or, even better, customers manoeuvring to be invited to the events you sponsor.

A few general points on measuring results:

- Try to check if the image you get through sponsorship is actually the one you desire. If you sponsor a prestigious, national and upmarket event, humble Joe Public may think you are a shade too mighty to want to deal with him.
- Avoid staying in an area for so long as a sponsor that you get better known for the activity than for what you do or sell (admittedly this is a problem many sponsors would be glad to have).
- If research suggests you have reached saturation or met your objectives, consider stopping at the end of the contract.
- If your research indicates that an entrepreneur involved in your sponsorship has a new swimming pool, but you haven't seen any improvement in your business affairs, move on.

Because of the wide ranging nature of sponsorship, measuring its effect is inevitably rather a grey area. No doubt as sponsorship grows more people will step forward claiming to be able to measure this and that accurately; just stay a shade sceptical.

At this point if you are a sponsor it is time to say goodbye because the rest of the book is directed at those seeking sponsorship. However, you may care to stay with us so that you understand some of the despair and deprivation behind the countless letters I am sure you get asking for support.

Part 2

How to Find and Keep Sponsorship

Chapter 15 **Groundwork**

If you have bought or, less commendably, borrowed this book because you seek sponsorship and have skipped Part 1, I'd like to suggest that you go back and read it because if you understand what motivates a sponsor you will have a more realistic chance of finding one. Anyway, if you're a sportsman you should understand a bit about business. You don't want to be a gorilla all your life do you? Another banana?

Attitude

If you are to have any chance of raising sponsorship it is vital that you approach the task with the right attitude. Recognize that sponsorship is not patronage, charity or benevolence but a fee for services rendered, and it should be a strictly two-way business deal under which you give something in return for support. Unless you tackle sponsorship with a clear understanding of this you are unlikely to find or keep it.

There are countless more people seeking sponsorship than there are sponsors, so accept that it will be hard work, and if you are not prepared to put effort into it you will not succeed. In fact being 'sponsor aware' is becoming an *essential* attribute for certain sportsmen, especially where high capital costs are involved. For instance of the many potential star racing drivers around, the ones who reach the top may well be those able to make sponsors enthusiastic.

Before you start your search, look in the mirror (force yourself) and ask yourself *why* you deserve sponsorship. You've condensed all of Shakespeare's plays into a one-hour mime? To be performed in the dark? And you want a sponsor for the LP? Or your drives to the supermarket in Fiona's Fiesta have convinced you that you have potential as a racing driver, and you'd like to move into Formula One? Praiseworthy aims indeed, but what possible benefits could sponsors get from supporting you? If *you* were a marketing director would you support such projects? Of course not.

I am not trying to deter you. I am trying to illustrate the pitfalls and the importance of the right attitude.

What do you need?

Anyway, having established a realistic approach to sponsorship, consider carefully why you need it. Could you solve your financial problems in other ways? Have you got expensive hi-fi equipment? Have you considered selling it to pay some of your bills? If not, is it because you are not sufficiently determined? If you don't burn with ambition maybe you won't make it anyway. If you are an event organizer, do you end up with empty seats? If so, wouldn't it be sensible to find ways to fill them before searching for finance elsewhere? Or would a one-off fund raising dinner be a better way of solving your problems than seeking sponsorship?

Incidentally, do accept that sponsorship-seeking is an enormous lottery and someone you know to be an inferior organizer or performer may get sponsorship through lucky breaks, while you fail; don't whine about your bad breaks and your rival's luck, just vow to try harder because those that do somehow seem to have the better luck.

The Sports Council publish an excellent guide for clubs called 'Fund Raising for Sport' in which sponsorship is only one of many ideas suggested, and the Arts Council have information sheets showing alternative sources of funding. (*Working for Yourself in the Arts and Crafts* by Sarah Hosking, published by Kogan Page, includes good advice on the arts subsidy network.) You should make full use of local advice too, as well as of any available grants. Bear in mind that you will be approaching businessmen who may not be impressed if you have failed to take full advantage of what is going. For the same reason, your financial calculations (covered later) need to be businesslike.

The percentage of your needs which has to be found from sponsorship will affect your approach to the task. If you need 100 per cent, you are clearly on very marginal ground; if you need only 20 per cent of funding from outside sources then things are healthier and in such a case you should guard against 20 per cent of your revenue occupying 80 per cent of your time in servicing a demanding sponsor. The happiest arrangement is being able to use sponsorship to pay for additional events which can be dropped if you lose support.

Irrespective of the size of the sponsorship contribution, do vow to keep control of your activity; event organizers may of course tailor their timing to suit a sponsor but don't prostitute an activity totally (a good sponsor wouldn't expect you to anyway).

Even if you don't need any funding, you should still consider taking sponsorship because of the additional promotional push which a sponsor can give; just the influence wielded by a sponsor, plus his business know-how, may be a help at times.

In establishing your needs you may prefer to try to get help in kind. Some people may prefer to give goods or assign people to help rather than pay cash, but don't become known as a sponger; some annual dinners have menu cards, meals, tombola prizes, even cabarets and guest speakers sponsored, which may all be fine but the line between value-for-money sponsorship and blackmail gets a bit indistinct on such occasions.

Organization

The competition for sponsorship is so intense that whether you are an individual or a large group, you must get organized. And whether amateur or professional in your sport or art-form, you must be professional in your approach to sponsorship. If you are not organized, wake up; sponsorship is now firmly part of the scene. Get organized for it. (This does not mean you need huge committees on the task; one person with flair may be more effective.)

Treat finding sponsorship as a marketing campaign, not charitable fund-raising. Companies – well, some of them – plan years ahead while budgets for a coming year will invariably be locked up by August so develop your approach well ahead too. And also plan your financial affairs long-term; don't delay looking for funds until you hit a cash flow crisis because you will fare better if potential sponsors cannot see the fear of bankruptcy in your eyes.

The need for planning means that events need to be arranged early; even critics of the insidious effects of sponsorship will perhaps accept that it is tending to bring a more disciplined approach to event calendars. (Unless you do plan events well ahead there will be little chance of TV coverage.)

Activities will have more chance of sponsorship if they are seen to have their act together; squabbles between individuals and associations, or between local and national organizations, are less than endearing. For that reason, sports in particular should be clear on who retains what slice of the sponsorship cake for sanctioned events.

Businessmen may not expect amateurs to have corporate structures but they will be more impressed if approached by people who seem to know what they are doing. And there is no harm in scattering a few job titles around – 'Sponsorship Manager' or 'Marketing Executive' may look better printed on the notepaper or typed below your name than 'Assistant Social Secretary' or whatever.

The better known you are, the better chance you will have of sponsorship, so build links to the media. Organizations should have press officers, while individuals should keep in mind that if they don't tell the press what they are doing, no one else may. Not a time for false modesty.

Long term, unless you are properly geared to sponsorship, you are unlikely to retain it. As an example, if you have a magazine or programme editor, he must know exactly what has been agreed with sponsors so that he avoids clashing advertising. And by the way, it is not a bad idea to keep an eye on what the opposition are up to. If you don't and they initiate a whole new league or festival series with a major sponsor, they could drastically affect your life.

Agents and agencies

You may decide to use an agent to help your search for sponsorship. If so, do tread carefully. A small but apparently growing number of sponsors are reluctant to deal through middlemen as they themselves gain confidence in the field, although in such cases an agent could operate behind the scenes advising you, drafting letters for your signature and so on. (An agency will fulfil much the same role as an agent for someone seeking sponsorship but may be able to offer more comprehensive support in-house.)

If you are new to sponsorship, or are breaking into new territory, an agent should be able to steer you through the many pitfalls and, if you are modest, will be more able to shout your wares. If as an individual you grow into a big star then an agent may be even more necessary, if nothing else to remind you which sponsor's cap fits in which country. But again: caution. Over-sharp agents can build up hostility and there are examples of stars who have been virtually sidelined through greedy managers demanding more than the market would bear.

The best way of finding an agent is by word of mouth. Ask around people in a similar field and then, if what you have to offer is substantial enough, consider asking two or three agents to pitch for your business. If you finally appoint one to act for you, be very clear on the conditions. Consider such things as:

- What are the terms of payment? Is the agent to get a flat fee or operate on commission? If the latter, is it on what you receive from the sponsor or on *all* your revenue?

- How long is the agent to search for sponsorship for you and is he or she to have an exclusive contract? It may be wise to give an agent an exclusive for so many weeks or months to get his undivided attention but the risk is that, if he then fails, time may be running out for you to find support elsewhere.

- What expenses will you have to meet? You may decide that if an agent searches in his own country, he pays his own expenses but if he travels abroad then you meet costs but only with prior agreement when you have established that the particular lead is really worth following up. It doesn't matter what the system is provided it is clear. If you are too generous you may simply be paying for an agent to have a jolly time phoning then wining and dining old pals in various marketing jobs.

- Establish who pays for any lavish brochures, advertisements and so on. It may not be unreasonable that you should do so – after all you need to invest to gain sponsorship – but if an agent is to get a healthy commission (again this is up to you to negotiate but it may range from 10 to 25 per cent) he should expect to stand some of the risk.

- Set out just what will be acceptable to you and if you are not prepared to take, say, a foreign company as a sponsor then say so at the start otherwise an agent may, rightly, claim expenses (or even sue you) if he finds a willing sponsor who you then reject.

- Recognize that it will be difficult to sue an agent for lack of success in finding sponsorship; the courts have little experience to go on and an agent would find it fairly easy to demonstrate that he had made an effort.

Incidentally, if an agent is particularly persistent in trying to get your business, you may find that asking for a firm guarantee of what he will produce will stop the phone calls.

Finally, if you appoint an agent (or agency) don't assume that your problems are solved. Keep in touch with him, feed him leads and generally take an interest. If you don't, and the fee potential from you is small, you may be filed and forgotten.

What have you got to offer?

If you engage an agent you should involve him totally in your campaign, not least in analysing what you have to sell to a sponsor and how to package it. If you are operating on your own, you should sit back and consider all the delights your activity offers. Caution: no doubt you are besotted with whatever you do, but don't assume everyone else will be. Try to take a detached view. Can things be improved? If you have a hospitality unit to offer sponsors, is it becoming a shade scruffy? If so, a few pounds and hours spent with a tin of emulsion before you show it to a potential sponsor may be a wise investment. Or can the staging of your event be changed to appeal more to sponsors without destroying its integrity?

Although you should be realistic in analysing what you are offering, you should naturally present everything in the best possible light. If yours is the largest, biggest, fastest, brightest or whatever, say so. Accept that sponsors will not be keen to support controversial activities or to contribute simply to general running costs such as salaries. You may need something more visible to offer them and, for instance, a museum is more likely to raise sponsorship if it stages a specific event or happening to which a company name can be linked.

Consider what your particular activity can do for a sponsor and, to help you prepare your presentation package, jot down all the things you have to offer. They may include the following:

- A sponsor's name included in an event or team title.
- Facilities to entertain customers.
- A specific number of events (with a wide geographical spread perhaps?).
- A guaranteed number of free tickets for all events and special discounted rates for more.
- Visits to sponsors' premises by stars.
- Priority bookings at events for sponsors' employees (with special prices?).
- A guaranteed number of banners at events.
- So many free pages of advertising in programmes and yearbooks, plus guaranteed editorial coverage.

- Television coverage.
- Links with local radio stations.
- Regular press releases (and newsletters?).
- If you can persuade a local or national newspaper to confirm that it will refer to the sponsor, then specifically mention this and perhaps include a letter from the editor in your package.
- Space at events for product displays.
- Availability of stars and sponsored hardware for in-store promotions.
- Enhanced community relations if there is a local activity to support.
- Publicity through stickers, posters, tickets, books, videos etc, plus the possibility of sales kiosks for these at events.
- A strong appeal to a particular market segment. And if you are not aware which people your activity attracts, shame on you. Sponsors will need an indication of spectators' age, sex and social class. Add other details if available such as how far people travel to events and if they do so by car. Many businessmen seem fascinated by research and in this area anything will be better than nothing. I am not suggesting that you should make figures up, but even the results of a simple questionnaire handed out at an event may help. The actual figures may not be all that meaningful – what will impress is the fact that you have made an effort. It will show that you appreciate a sponsor's needs.
- Sponsors' decals on competitors' clothing.
- Opportunities for the sale of team clothing.
- Stress any unusual opportunities you can offer – photographs of sponsors' clients chatting to stars or playing golf with them, or their children having a privileged coaching session. In other words, anything which would not normally be readily available – it is the unique things in sponsorship which make it such an effective area.

Point out that there will be goodwill and other benefits simply from a link with a bright activity like yours; you may need to 'sell' this side of sponsorship to someone new to it who is familiar with a more orderly (and duller?) marketing arena.

Consider 'pairing' your offerings putting, say, a youth scheme alongside something involving your stars, or if you have an item for which it is rather difficult to find sponsorship then link this with one of your more attractive offerings.

The guarantee of TV coverage will dramatically improve your

chances of finding a sponsor and, if you are an event organizer, you may get revenue from television itself. In the growth stages of an activity it is worth pleading and bending over backwards to get it covered by TV because if it then attracts viewers you may command television fees for future coverage. In fact, in the case of an activity previously untelevised (such as a sport) it may be worth investing to encourage TV coverage by creating a fighting fund, to which participants and sponsors contribute, which is used to pay for an independent company to cover events; a worthwhile TV outlet needs sorting out in advance, of course. Such arrangements need some care and should ideally be arranged by a central organizing body – such as a national association – because if it is left to individuals there may be squabbles over 'who paid how much for what' or, far more serious, adverse press coverage about the ethics of the whole business.

If you obtain TV coverage don't relax and assume that they will go on turning up or coughing up forever because viewing patterns change, new activities emerge and unless you stay alert your burst of screen stardom may be short-lived.

One final point about listing what you have to offer a sponsor: don't promise what you can't deliver. If organizers are not certain that they can persuade all entrants to carry a sponsor's name or individuals are not sure that they can take part in a specific number of events, they should not say so. Disillusionment can destroy sponsorship.

Finance

If you have considered all the delights you have for sponsors, now comes the hard part. What do you charge? To help your thought process, consider the following:

- The fee should really be what the package is worth to a sponsor and related to what the market will stand, *not* what you so desperately need. The majority of sponsorship seekers quote what they need to run a programme and, surprisingly, most sponsors seem to accept this approach but it is quite wrong if you think about it.
- To some extent, what you can charge will depend on how well regarded your particular activity is at the time; for instance, it is not ideal to sell football sponsorship the morning after a riot.
- It may be worse to ask too little than too much. You can

negotiate downwards but you will rarely be able to raise a figure.

- Try to relate the cost *to* something, eg 'that is less than four half-page ads in the local newspaper'.
- If you are negotiating with company personnel remember that it is not their money they are handing over. This may sometimes make them more generous.
- If you find haggling distressing and embarrassing then consider using an agent.
- Don't be over-optimistic when budgeting. If half-way through a project you are forced to take your bucket to the sponsorship well again, you may find it dries up altogether the following year.

Should you quote a figure in your initial presentation? There are mixed views. If it is a small project or a significant one which can be broken down into component parts, each with a price, then most sponsors will be glad to have figures stated. For major schemes involving national TV and so on the figure is best left for discussion at meetings.

Even if you quote figures in your initial presentation, don't drown people in detail. If you are seeking sponsorship for a dance project you don't really need to itemize the laundry and embrocation bills. However, do have detailed budgets and cash flow forecasts available as back-up when you get to the discussion stage; sponsors may not be interested in the detail but they will be comforted to see that you appear to be in control of your affairs.

If you have sat back and established just what you have to offer sponsors, let us move on to consider how to present the material.

Chapter 16 **The Search**

Having assembled your ammunition, you need to fire it so that it grabs potential sponsors' attention in the flood of approaches which companies receive. Most executives prefer the initial approach to be via a letter and/or brochure rather than a telephone call and all letters should be typed, preferably on headed paper. Photocopied letters deserve photocopied replies (if any) so don't send them. The use of a word processor may speed the process for you but do try to personalize your letters, and not just in the topping and tailing – tailor at least part of the contents to each potential sponsor too.

Don't bore people by telling them more about your proposal in a letter than they really need to know; better to have a fairly brief, punchy one with more details in an enclosure such as a brochure.

Design

Give careful thought to the design of a brochure and try to tailor it to reflect the quality and flavour of what you are offering and also, as far as possible, to what people may be expecting from you. This balance is important because a scruffy uninformative package will suggest you are inefficient, while an over-elaborate and obviously expensive publication for a relatively low-cost project may imply that you have more money then sense and therefore do not need or deserve further help. If you have access to tame designers then by all means get them involved in creating your brochure but with the caveat that they should not go over the top. It is worthwhile obtaining presentations by other activities to study what standards you have to beat or at least match. You may decide to take an offbeat approach in presenting your case. For instance, Lincolnshire and Humberside Arts cover '10 reasons for not taking the subject seriously' and then effectively go on to demolish all the common arguments against sponsorship (their booklet is itself sponsored of course).

It may be too time-consuming and difficult to create a separate brochure for each company you approach, but do keep in mind the general sort of person you are trying to reach; you will not go far wrong if you assume that they are busy people, so avoid waffle. Don't have long tedious paragraphs but instead keep them short (and number them). Get to the point early in your contents because if you start with a three-page history of your association you will lose your readers; if you must have a three-page history (and I can't think why) then put it as an appendix.

Don't assume that the people you are approaching share your enthusiasm for, or knowledge of, your activity, so don't use jargon which they won't understand.

Include all the plus points collated in the previous chapter, put them in rough priority order and add the following information where relevant:

- A brief paragraph on your organization: when it started, how many members, names of key officials, long-term objectives and plans (if any). In other words enough to show that it is stable and has a place in the local or national scene.
- Give previous attendance figures at events you have run, provided they are reasonably significant.
- Mention any awards you or your organization have won.
- Include a montage of any press coverage you have had.
- Mention any other sponsors you have or have had, and if they are prepared to act as referees then say so.
- If you have a video of your activities, either enclose a copy if you can afford it or mention that one is available, then take it with you if you get to the interview stage.

Be upbeat in your approach and do choose your words with care; if you are presenting some brave way-out project then refer to it as 'innovative' rather than 'controversial'. If you have an artist to hand, prepare an illustration showing how your offering could be decorated in a potential sponsor's colours, but handle logos and house-styles with care because companies can get very touchy about them. It may be better to take such sketches along at the interview stage so that you can explain the rationale behind them.

Having drafted a telling letter and a selling document make a final check that you are being realistic. Your approach must be honest; you needn't be apologetic because you are, or should be, offering something of value but you shouldn't lie and you shouldn't promise something you know you simply can't deliver. Then get your draft documents vetted by a hard-nosed businessman, ideally someone used to receiving such presentations.

Consider carefully how many copies of the letter and brochure you will need and endeavour to get sponsorship from a printer. But above all, *don't* assume your problems are now over. There is a tendency to relax when a brochure comes back from the printers as if a major peak has been climbed. Not so, because thousands of other people will be busy preparing very similar documents. (Can you think of anything which will help to make your proposal stand out?)

Contacts

Perhaps more important than the design of your brochure is what you actually do with it. Obviously, you want to use it to attract sponsors, but first consider if there are any sponsors you *don't* want. For instance:

- An organization should be cautious in linking with sponsors with tarnished reputations. Run a bank and shareholders' check on unknown companies.
- People seeking sponsorship should decide early on if there are specific areas they will not consider, for instance there may be a reason for not linking with foreign companies.
- If you are sponsored by one newspaper or magazine, others may ignore you or give you minimal coverage. This may not matter but you should be aware of the risk.
- Although 'trade' sponsorship may be available (from companies in the same field) it may be healthier to look wider for sponsorship; certainly you will extend the media coverage if you go outside a cloistered world.
- You may need to be rather circumspect if approaching employers for support. Some may like to leap on your bandwagon, others may question whether your mind is really on the job for which they pay you.

Having considered who not to solicit, you can now be more positive and start approaching people. Despite modern marketing methods the most effective way of getting sponsorship is still through the old pals' network and members of an organization (or friends of an individual seeking support) should draw up lists of who they know and they should spread the net as widely as possible. Peer pressure can work to raise sponsorship if one director talks to another, and 'peer' pressure may help too if you can list one on your headed paper to add stature.

However, even if you gain access to a potential sponsor through the grapevine, it is still worth having a brochure about your plans as an indication that you are serious. In any case, unless it is a small sum for a pet project, many bosses may prefer to have a proposal vetted by colleagues before committing. And do remember the risk if you gain sponsorship through a contact and the contact leaves: his successor, in sweeping clean, may brush you away too, much in the way advertising agencies often get fired at such macho moments.

If you fail through the old boys' network then, before you start mailing your brochure to all and sundry, consider other tacks, for instance:

- Hold a series of meetings (perhaps lunches) for potential sponsors at which you make a presentation and give them a chance to ask questions. Have copies of the brochure for them to take away.
- Project yourself at exhibitions and trade and town shows to attract sponsors. Consider a simple leaflet as a bulk hand-out with brochures for more serious prospects.
- Advertise in the marketing magazines for sponsorship (but don't make your ads as desperately plaintive as many of them tend to be).
- Consult local trade groups for advice such as the Chamber of Commerce and regional offices of the CBI and Institute of Directors.
- Consider approaching your town (it has worked for ice skaters) or even a town it is twinned with.

In other words, use your initiative and imagination.

However, if all the hyperactivity has failed to find a sponsor and your mum is starting to moan about the pile of brochures in the back bedroom, what should you do next? Draw up a prospect list.

Spend time in a library working through local trade directories and phone books as well as books like *The Times 1000* and *Who Owns Whom*. Study the financial and marketing press and watch the business and sports pages of newspapers for opportunities. And add advertising and PR agencies to your list.

You may, too easily, end up with an optimistically long list of names and addresses but . . . be realistic. Sit down with the list and consider which companies are *really* likely to benefit from a link with you; make them your priority, tailoring your letters accordingly. Don't be totally conventional in this analysis but apply lateral thinking and see if you can think of a link which, by being unusual, may attract interest. If the sifting process still leaves you with a large number of companies then, if you have the manpower, consider a small team with each member responsible for contacting up to, say, 10 companies. This may add to the impact by encouraging a little rivalry, although such schemes must be well coordinated. There must be regular liaison meetings, if nothing else to keep up morale because if you approach 100 companies you may be invited to visit five, of which one will take up your proposal (if you are lucky); most won't bother to reply, while some will assume your letter is a request for charity and send you a fiver. It's a cruel world.

Be disciplined. Keep a log of what letters are sent and received and, although it is not as important as sometimes suggested, it is still worth making the effort to address letters to individuals by name. Phone companies and ask telephonists who handles sponsorship; if they don't know then the PR or marketing departments should. If nobody knows then you've either got a problem or a splendid opportunity. Phone calls may also help you to establish if sponsorship is handled locally or by a head office further away; policies on this vary. Local branches may have lower sign-off limits but try to get them interested (even if only at an informal level) before you approach head office staff; the latter are likely to consult their local branch before deciding and the locals may say 'no' out of pique if they have not been consulted by you.

Many people selling things (as you will be) write something along the lines of 'I will call your secretary to make an appointment in a few days'. Often this simply alerts executives to tell their secretaries to say that they are out but nevertheless some form of follow-up is essential and if you don't get a reply within, say, 10 days, phone to try to get an appointment. Sure, in following up hard you run the risk of irritating some people but others may actually be impressed by your persistence. If you don't follow up, you certainly won't get anywhere. A stamped addressed envelope is not really necessary unless you specifically want a brochure returned. Above all, regard the letters, brochures and any follow-up phone calls mainly as ways of arranging a meeting with a company.

Face to face

If you are invited to meet a company to discuss sponsorship then prepare and above all, try to see your project from *their* point of view. Get the company's annual accounts and any other literature it produces because this will give you a clue to how image conscious they are. What is their marketing style? Would sponsorship fit in? It would be sensible to study what they make or do, and you should try to establish where the company is in its life: is it on an upswing or has it got problems? If the latter, are they ones that sponsorship might ease? A community relations problem might be helped by sponsoring a local activity for example. Has the company sponsored anything before? If so, was it successful? If you know the people who were sponsored and they are not rivals, call them for background information and a guide to possible pitfalls.

Try to establish if those you will be meeting can actually make decisions; what you may think is agreement may just mean that the decision is to be referred up a very tall tree. Even if you make someone in a company enthusiastic, he may still have quite an internal fight to get agreement; inter-company rivalries may have a part to play as may the chairman's hobby. The lesson is not to mistake polite interest for cast-iron acceptance.

Having found out as much as possible about the company you are to visit, your negotiating party should get itself organized and, I suggest, establish how long the meeting is scheduled for and then rehearse what is to be said and who is to say it. If the hard-nosed businessman mentioned earlier is still around, ask him to sit through a rehearsal of your proposed presentation and then to throw awkward questions at you so that you are armed and well prepared.

Select your party with care and don't go mob handed because a sponsor will not be impressed at being outnumbered, particularly if he himself has been laying off staff. One person should be in charge, while if a member of your group is a bit abrasive or obsessive and likely to annoy people then leave him at home. Company decision-makers will not take kindly to being harangued and (ye gods this is delicate ground) many companies are still male-dominated and may take even less kindly to being lectured by a shrill-voiced harpy.

Your negotiators should be reasonably well dressed although not necessarily in pinstripes; designer jeans may be fine, but designer dirt under the fingernails may have less appeal.

Take plenty of copies of your proposal plus additional material to flesh out your case, such as a more detailed financial budget perhaps – anything to help indicate that you are organized and not dreaming. And talking of finance, do be clear exactly what you are going to say in answer to the question, 'What do you want the money for?'

Vow not to waste people's time but do consider taking visual aids; you may have a few (repeat few) slides which effectively illustrate what you have to offer or it may be appropriate to show a film or video. Another suitable visual aid could be a drawing of a venue showing banner sites, TV camera positions (if known) and so on. If you can get people interested through such visuals you will be well on the way to selling your proposal, but don't make the presentation a long drawn out affair with people struggling to make projectors work (get the technical equipment sorted out before the meeting). Incidentally, if you have drawings or even models illustrating how things would look in a sponsor's colours, do leave them with the company because they may help the internal selling process.

Don't ramble in your presentation and don't gabble away through nerves but do make an effort, and be positive in highlighting the strengths of what you have. If you make a good presentation, the impact may be dramatic through being unexpected, particularly if people from the arts world are concerned, where a certain ethereal vagueness may be anticipated.

If the company doesn't know much about your activity, spell out exactly what is included in the deal, as well as any significant items not included, to avoid confusion and discord later. If you are too vague they may think that they are getting the Boat Race when you are actually offering them a local canoeing contest.

During any general discussion at a meeting, try to probe a company's objectives in sponsoring and if they haven't really got any (more likely than you may think) encourage them to create some, making sure that they are ones which your sponsorship will enable them to meet.

Be flexible and think on your feet during a meeting but don't glibly agree to add another event to what you know is an already crowded calendar (you will just get tired and lack-lustre stars) and if you have budgeted carefully, don't settle for less if you know you won't be able to complete the agreed programme. For all these reasons it is important that the negotiating party agree in advance just how far they are prepared (or allowed by a committee perhaps) to give way to clinch a deal; it may be possible to link two projects together at a special price for a sponsor.

Other points:

- Don't expect quick decisions.
- If a company is new to sponsorship you may find it reluctant to sign up long term.
- If you find a frivolous sponsor for a one-off, don't expect such 'fun money' to stay involved long term.
- Recognize that the prevailing reputation of the activity you are involved in may influence a company as much as the charm of the particular piece you are touting.
- Don't criticize or gossip about other sponsors during a meeting.
- If hospitablity is offered, don't descend on it like gannets; stop short of asking for a doggybag even if you are starving through lack of funds.
- Don't whinge about 'no one will support me'. You won't be seen as unlucky but simply as a whinger.

End a meeting on a positive note and be clear who will be doing what; don't be vague on the arrangements.

If, sadly, you are turned down there and then, don't become abusive but do try to establish the reason for the rejection. If it is through circumstances beyond your control – such as a clash with company policy – then so be it, but if you sense it is because of a poor presentation then ask for criticisms so that you can improve next time.

After a meeting, write a 'thank you for seeing me' letter and, if things are still in play, use this to reinforce any weak points or answer any questions raised.

You may have no alternative but to juggle negotiations with several potential sponsors at once because if every company takes, say, a month to decide on your package (and it will probably be longer) then after two have turned you down you may be running out of time. However, the negotiating team should be clear on who is handling what; be wary of trying to hurry a company into a decision by saying you have someone else interested because they may simply call your bluff and say 'no'.

Legal

If you finally find support, do put things in writing even if the sponsor himself seems happy with a handshake. It need only be a friendly letter setting out the key points but have something in case any of the negotiating parties leave the scene. You should be totally clear on payment terms to avoid future embarrassment and if, say, you have agreed that the sponsor can market goods carrying your name then insist on a quality control role for you or an associate.

A written agreement is most important where several sponsors are concerned otherwise they may spend the duration of the sponsorship bickering over who gets what and when.

If an involved project is being considered, you should have legal people vet an agreement on your behalf so that you are clear what happens if, say, the sponsor goes bankrupt during the agreement; it is most unlikely that people could sue you for a sponsor's debts or defective goods, but it is worth a legal look. If you are a rising young star, avoid being pressured into signing over-long contracts with agents or managers; the flesh market in young talent is one of the less savoury results of the growth of sponsorship.

Finally, although sponsors may be reluctant to take you to court if you don't deliver, you should not enter an agreement with any sharp thoughts of taking advantage of their relaxed approach. There is a sponsors' grapevine and word will soon spread that you don't travel well.

Chapter 17 **Keeping a Sponsor**

Having found sponsors, don't heave a sigh of relief because your financial problems are solved, then forget all about them. Don't take sponsors for granted but instead, work to retain them; after all, if (as is likely) you had a hell of a struggle to find support, you don't want to go through it all again in a year's time do you? Apart from all the hassle, swopping sponsors every year can be destabilizing for an activity.

The kind of sponsor you net may affect what sort of a time you have; a sharp operator in a keenly competitive business field may demand more than his pound of flesh, whereas you may need to gently nudge a more relaxed sponsor to ensure that he gets value.

Whoever the sponsor, the best way to retain him is to start with all parties clearly understanding the arrangements; there should be no ambiguity. Establish who your day-to-day contact is within the sponsoring company to ensure a smooth working relationship and, not least, to avoid stumbling into intra-company rivalries.

You on your side should assign someone to look after a sponsor and play a key role as a bridge between the two sides. It is the liaison man's task to see that sponsors get satisfaction without disrupting the success of the project being sponsored. Often, a steering committee will be desirable with all interested parties represented on it.

Have a plan with a detailed timetable and try to stick to it; companies will, or should, be fairly organized in their approach to life so try to avoid giving them any surprises (the same goes for your bank manager during the sponsorship). Be realistic; don't promise what you can't deliver and if there are any enforced changes to your plan then confirm them in writing. In fact it is sensible to write after any meetings to confirm (briefly) what has been agreed; keep such correspondence on a friendly plane, of course.

You should take particular care over the press side because if you blab about some good news in an eager desire to help your sponsors, you may simply foul up a carefully laid PR plan by premature disclosure. Both sides should be clear who is to prepare, sign off and issue press releases about the sponsorship. Know too who is to organize hospitality.

Obviously, financial arrangements should be carefully spelt out; keep financial records and make them available to a sponsor on request. If you are to be paid by instalments then the first will probably need to be the largest to cover setting up or buying equipment, but don't expect to get a cheque the day after you've agreed the link; companies are rarely that quick at paying. Many companies have a fast track system for urgent payments; it may be wise or even essential to get on to those particular rails for all your cheques. Start biting your nails if the first payment takes longer than, say, a month to arrive and start kneading your knuckles over the last cheque if either the link has not been a wild success or you have found you have been working with a rather sharp operator.

Having sorted out the guidelines right at the start, do involve the sponsor as the programme progresses. Be friendly and try to form a good working partnership. If you are in the arts world don't patronize a sponsor even if he clearly finds *EastEnders* an intellectual challenge or suggests getting taller ballet dancers to save yours having to stand on their toes. The more you make a sponsor part of your world, the more you are likely to keep him. And don't forget that once he appears on your particular artistic or sporting scene, he will be vulnerable to poaching by other people. You in turn will be polite to other people's sponsors, won't you? (Not for any ulterior motive, you understand.)

Your liaison man, or you yourself if you are a one-man band, should contact sponsors at frequent intervals and, for instance, invite them to training sessions, rehearsals or whatever your particular activity has to offer so that they feel involved.

After events, send sponsors brief reports plus results, whether of box office takings or race positions; do this whether the news is good or bad. A more elaborate report in the form of a newsletter to go to customers and others will be desirable for many links. Novice sponsors may confuse such activity with media coverage, which will be no bad thing, although you should be aiming for real media coverage too and you should work closely with sponsors to achieve it. Don't hesitate to draw their attention to possible stories and other opportunties to promote the link. Keep press clippings and see that sponsors get them and do encourage the press to acknowledge your sponsors.

If you have several sponsors you will need to work even harder and display considerable tact in balancing their interests. Consider encouraging them to form a small working party to ensure close liaison. *Don't* try to play one sponsor off against another; *never* criticize a sponsor publicly but *do* try to make them all feel a bit special; you don't have to be obsequious but you do have to make them feel wanted. Try to give more than was negotiated and, for instance, if a link is working well, why not make the sponsor's chief executive an honorary this or that? Let it be a surprise and make it clear that it is a unique honour you are bestowing. Such things needn't cost much, just a little initiative and the right attitude to sponsorship (which must be two-way, because sponsorship is a fee for services rendered: or had you forgotten already?).

Plan carefully, spend sponsors' money wisely and then, in plenty of time, make an approach for the following year or season. Even if the sponsor says 'no' he may, if you have worked hard, be able to steer you to other business contacts as potential sponsors.

All rather a lot of work? Agreed, but unless you accept that that is what sponsorship entails then even if you find it, you won't retain it.

It may be wise to end with a few notes of caution:

- Don't let sponsorship blind you to other ways of balancing your books. Try not to become lazy and totally dependent on sponsors.
- Working hard to involve sponsors does not mean you should let them take over and totally dictate to you, hence the importance of clear groundrules from the start.
- Perhaps most essential of all, don't let the sponsorship deter you from your main aim. If you are an athlete then winning is all, even if it does mean missing a sponsor's banquet the night before a race; if you don't do what you should do well, then in the long term you won't be very attractive to sponsors anyway.

Way back at the beginning of this book I said that an added advantage of sponsorship over other marketing activities is that it can be fun. But it isn't fun if there are squabbles over who said this and that, so let me close the chapter with a final and, I hope, not forlorn plea: be reliable and keep your word.

Chapter 18 Charities

So far this book has been directed at business people considering sponsorship, and at people in sports and the arts seeking support; this final chapter is for those raising funds for purely charitable purposes, although many of the points apply equally to social clubs and associations looking for assistance. As there are several benefits in having charitable status, such groups may wonder if they qualify. Well, to be able to register with the Charity Commissioners, an organization must satisfy certain conditions, among which are the following:

- The aims must fall under one or more of the activities which are considered charitable, namely: relief of the poor; advancement of education; advancement of religion and, finally, other purposes beneficial to the community (and defined as such by the court). The latter covers such things as protection of health, animals and the environment, help for the disabled and the old.
- Any profit or income must be used for charitable purposes.
- Charities must not have political objectives (although some of them embark on political lobbying).

As you will observe, sports associations would probably not qualify, although many arts groups as well as preservation societies, parent–teacher associations and the like would. If a group feels it could become a charity it should contact the Charity Commissioners for the necessary forms to complete.

As sponsorship becomes increasingly fashionable, charities may consider calling donors 'sponsors' and creating special titles for more generous folk – 'Gold Sponsors' or whatever. But as well as receiving funds from such traditional donors, a charity can be sponsored just like any other activity, giving something in return for funding. As sponsorship of sport and the arts becomes saturated, companies may increasingly turn to full-blooded sponsorship of charitable projects, to their own benefit and to the benefit of charities which are sufficiently alert to the changing scene itself to seize the opportunities. A charity may even consider being a sponsor to raise funds while promoting its name. As employees are now allowed to give up to £120 per annum to charity out of pre-tax income (provided an employer agrees to operate a payroll scheme) the interest in giving is likely to grow and the charities with the highest profiles are likely to reap the golden harvests, provided they are organized. This will be essential because while a dithering, casual approach may once have appeared rather charming, now it would seem time-wasting, lazy and undeserving of support. If you are the secretary of a small social group quietly minding your own business, you may wonder if you really need such a go-go approach; maybe not, but if you don't keep in touch with trends then don't be surprised if younger members form livelier splinter groups.

One happy result of linking with a business sponsor may be an improvement in your own efficiency as an organization, and if that means you become leaner and faster on your feet, all well and good, because perhaps the biggest problem charities face in finding sponsorship is convincing people that they are professional and can deliver what they promise. To too many potential sponsors, charities may still convey visions of tins being shaken on flag days.

To digress for what I hope will be a fruitful moment, I have talked to fund managers on the receiving end of charitable appeals and they recommend that the following points should be watched by those seeking donations or sponsorship:

1. Give your address and make your signature legible.
2. Avoid stereotyped or duplicated letters. And don't address a letter to Company A in which you refer throughout to the products of Company B.
3. If you attempt a personal approach, make sure the addressee is still in office and get his name and title right.
4. Keep your covering letter brief but include good attachments giving the details.
5. Don't bury your punchline; your letter, being one of hundreds, may only be skimmed.
6. Don't be condescending. Don't put 'the story of such-and-such is well known' if it isn't.
7. Be specific in what you are going to do with any money and state how much you have raised already (if relevant).

Don't supply so many sums and so much financial detail that you confuse the issue.

8. Don't appear to have set yourself an impossible task.
9. Answer letters with follow-up questions promptly; don't delay for weeks or ignore them altogether.
10. If potential donors or sponsors visit you, make it easy for them to find you and do turn the radio off when talking to them.

A silly list? You'd never make such elementary mistakes? So how come I was given examples of every one of them being made by charities which you would readily recognize? Is it any wonder some charities have problems convincing business people that they are professional? Guard against such howlers yourself.

But to return to the main body of my sermon, charities seeking sponsorship should, like anyone else, analyse just what they have to offer and then package it in the most attractive way. However, charities should take care with the design of brochures – they should be professional but not so lavish as to suggest there is money to waste. As well as including the sort of information suggested in Chapter 15, it is worth mentioning what percentage of revenue goes on overheads and if this is a high figure, perhaps it is time to question why.

Virtually anything can be sponsored and bear in mind an earlier point that it is easier to get support for specific projects or events than for general funds. The more amusing or unusual a scheme, the more likely it is to catch the imagination and money of a sponsor. And if a project is also fun you have more chance of getting celebrities to take part, which should swell the take.

Agents

You may decide to use an agent or professional fund-raiser to help you. Well, if so, take just as much care, perhaps even more, than advised earlier for businessmen.

When contacting agents note their response and the way they handle themselves because this will be an indication of how they will appear to potential supporters. Study their client list; check if they have previous experience in charitable work and be sure to meet the actual staff who will be working on your account. Ask agents to outline their proposed methods of soliciting sponsorship or raising funds for you. Do you approve of these methods? A nitpicking point? No; overhard sells are irritating and may damage a charity's reputation. It is all a question of balance: *of course* you must be single-minded in trying to reach targets but you should aim to do so without the whole population fervently wishing that you would go away.

When you have selected an agent, be careful to spell out in writing the arrangements under which they are to operate – what they can and can't commit on your behalf for instance, plus the financial terms. Consultants are likely to charge fees for feasibility studies then, when a campaign is underway, they may work for a fee or on commission; the latter may give them more incentive to try. Ideally, cheques from sponsors or donors should be made payable to a charity, who should receive *all* the money then pay an agent; people may be suspicious or inhibited otherwise.

Rogue agencies have been known to produce souvenir programmes from which only a tiny percentage of the revenue goes to the worthy causes, others have gone conveniently bankrupt after a major fundraising drive (before passing on the proceeds of course). Or you may hear of companies bandying your name about to raise funds or forming organizations which they pass off as yours. Add to these horrors the charmers who set up 'captive' charities which just, but only just, stay within the law and you will appreciate why you should be cautious. Let me stress that I am not suggesting that all fundraising agents are crooks, far from it. But dishonest ones make the headlines and if your charity is linked with one you too may get bad publicity; at the very least you will appear unworldly to have been duped.

You may have the manpower and knowledge to conduct your own affairs. If so, whether sponsoring or seeking sponsorship, do get everyone involved working to a plan; if you have regions or branches they must understand what they have to do and, just as important, what they must not do. Set out clear guidelines with proper control systems (particularly over cash) while if you have a 'Friends of . . .' organization helping, then be specific on its function; you may need to tread a fine and tactful line between a supportive role for it and an interfering and disruptive one.

Do recognize that charities need to take special care over sponsorship because they must be above reproach. They should, for instance, probe a potential sponsor's motives – he may wish to use the respectability of charitable sponsorship to cloak more nefarious activities. Charities should consider their own standards too when using sponsorship; as an example, many parents strongly resent the blackmail of their children through sponsored events, with badges and stickers as prizes, organized through schools. Schemes aimed at adults which have an element of moral blackmail can be equally unsavoury.

Trying to raise money for a worthwhile cause does not absolve you from paying attention to commonsense things like safety so, depending on what you are organizing, you may need to consider items such as age limits, first-aid cover, supervision, liaison with the police, control of litter and the many other problems which can arise. Back to being properly organized.

As well as guarding against danger or nuisance, you should also avoid confusion and this means having clear instructions for all concerned. And your follow-up should be sound too – a fun run for kids will be marred if they fail to receive the promised souvenir certificates afterwards. (As my children still remind me, cursing the sponsor as they so do, this marred an otherwise well-run roller skating event; the fact that it happened some considerable time ago illustrates how bad memories tend to linger.) Bear in mind too that donors are wary of open-ended commitments, therefore structure events so that they know what their maximum outlay is likely to be; let them put 'up to £x' if they wish for a fun run rather than so much per mile or blister.

Although sponsors may relax their normal commercial standards and caution if a charity is involved, this does not absolve you from giving value for money, particularly if you hope to work with a sponsor again. Equally, being a charity does not excuse anger or even abuse if you get turned down. Bob Geldof got away with the 'give me your (expletive deleted) money' approach; you may not.

A few final points:

- If you embark on joint promotions, whether for sponsorship or the sale of products, be very specific over the arrangements. Be sure that high expenses don't get siphoned off to a friend of a friend in cahoots.
- Take full advantage of convenants and any other money-saving methods – potential sponsors will not be impressed with your financial acumen if you fail to do so.
- If you find sponsorship and it leads to a cheque being handed over, maximize the press coverage (to encourage others to help you) even if the sponsor is modest. Then work hard to promote the sponsor throughout the link.

In other words, be businesslike – and do stay within the law.

Appendices

Appendix 1 Guidelines on Programmes Funded by Non-Broadcasters on Independent Television

1. When a programme is funded in whole or in part, directly or indirectly, by a commercial organization, the editorial content of the programme must not include any element of advertisement on behalf of the funder, and must not be directly related to the funder's commercial activities.
2. Responsibility for the content and scheduling of all programmes must rest with the broadcasters ie the programme company, and the IBA.
3. Credits may be given on screen to ITV companies, independent production companies and other broadcasting organizations who have financed a production. Acknowledgements to other funders of programmes need the IBA's approval.
4. Acknowledgements to other funders will only be considered when the programme consists, in the terms of the Broadcasting Act, of a factual portrayal of doings, happenings, places or things. This includes recordings or live relays of sporting, artistic and entertainment events which have an existence independent of the television broadcast itself. It may also include documentary programmes, but is not to be taken as including (i) programmes on matters of political or industrial controversy or relating to current public policy, or (ii) news programmes.
5. Acknowledgements may be in vision at the end, and, where considered appropriate, at the beginning also of the programme. Such acknowledgements may refer to brand as well as corporate names, but they may not include cigarette brand names or other products banned by the IBA Code from advertising. The wording must be agreed with the IBA in advance. The broadcasters reserve the right to impose restrictions on publicity in other media that the funder may wish to give to the programme.

6. When a programme contains an acknowledgement to a funder, advertisements containing that funder's name will normally be permitted within or around that programme, provided that there is no link in content or style with the programme. The Authority retains the right not to allow a funder's advertisements to be transmitted in or around a particular programme if it is judged that such transmissions could offend against Section 8 (6) and paragraph 1 of Schedule 2 of the Broadcasting Act 1981. Advertisements for products in competition with those of the programme funder will normally be acceptable with the proviso that there is no direct link in content or style with the programme.

7. Funding by non-broadcasters of coverage of events which themselves are sponsored is not permitted.

Quoted with permission.

Appendix 2 Cable Authority's Code of Practice on Programme Sponsorship

1. Types of sponsorship

A programme is deemed to be sponsored if any part of its costs of production or transmission is met by an organization or company other than a Cable Operator or recognized Programme Provider. For convenience operators and providers are referred to in this code as programmers.

Sponsored programmes may involve one or more of the following:

    (i) coverage of all or part of a sponsored event;
   (ii) supply to a programme maker of goods or services at less than wholesale cost;
  (iii) funding, in part or in total, of the costs of a programme's production or transmission.

These three broad categories of sponsorship are dealt with below in Sections 2–4.

2. Coverage of a sponsored event

    (i) Where (a) an event will take place regardless of whether it is covered in a cable programme, and (b) the full cost of coverage is met by the programmer, the programme is not deemed to be sponsored and the provisions of this Code do not apply. Other Authority Codes must still be observed (see section 5(i)).
   (ii) In all other cases, Section 4 (below) shall apply.

3. The supply of goods or services

    (i) Programme makers who accept goods or services from suppliers at less than wholesale cost may give an acknowledgement in sound or text at the beginning or end of the programme, which may include a brand name and a brief advertising copyline in support of the product. No undue prominence should be given in the programme to goods supplied in this way.

(ii) Prizes in game shows.
In addition to (i) (above), a second acknowledgement to the supplier may be given *once* during the programme. This acknowledgement may include a brand name but *not* a copyline.

(iii) Programmers may accept informational services at reduced or no charge in return for a screen acknowledgement to the information provider, which should appear in a proper proportion to the information displayed.

4. Funding by sponsors

Sponsors may provide funding to programmers in two ways:

(a) In a way that gives the sponsor no editorial involvement whatsoever (for example, by contributing to the costs of the acquisition of a previously-made programme, or by contributing to the costs of production of a cable programme where total editorial control rests with the programmer). This type of sponsorship is referred to below as *underwriting*.

(b) In a way that gives the sponsor editorial involvement, permitting him to exercise an influence over a programme's content or selection. This type of sponsorship is referred to below as *commissioning* (the ultimate form of commissioning would be where the sponsor provided a programme which he had made himself).

In either case, it is the programmer who is ultimately responsible for ensuring that the programme's content complies with the Authority's Codes.

(i) Underwriting
A sponsor who underwrites part or all of the cost of a cable programme must receive a credit immediately before or after the programme which may contain a short copyline.

(ii) Commissioning
A sponsor who commissions a cable programme must be credited in sound and text immediately before and after

the programme. Such a credit.

(a) may contain a short copyline;

(b) *must* use the word 'sponsored' in vision

(c) *must* detail for the viewer any of the sponsor's (or his associates') products, commercial activities or special interests not named which are relevant to the programme's subject matter. This information should be presented in a straightforward factual manner.

5. Application of other codes

(i) Programme Codes

All programmes, whether sponsored or not, are equally subject to the Authority's Code of Standards and Practice in Cable Programmes. Sponsored programmes should not, therefore, display any undue emphasis on the products, services or name of a sponsor or his associates. Where, in the Authority's opinion, a programme contains an undue element of advertisement it may be treated instead as an 'infomercial' and be subject to the Code of Advertising Standards and Practice ('the Advertising Code').

(ii) Sponsorship Credits

A sponsor's credit and any associated product copyline must comply (in terms of content) with the Advertising Code.

Credits may be inserted in breaks within a cable programme service at the discretion of the Programmer. Each insertion of a credit (with or without copyline) counts as advertising when determining the total advertising time on that service, with the exception of the mandatory credits required by Section 4 of this Code.

(iii) Spot Advertising

Programmers are free to offer sponsors spot advertising in breaks before, during or after the programme. All such advertising must observe the provisions of the Advertising Code.

6. Restricted/Prohibited sponsors and programmes

(i) Unacceptable Products

Goods or services which are excluded from cable advertising by the Advertising Code (eg cigarettes), are not acceptable for sponsorship, other than as described in Section 2 (i) (Coverage of Sponsored Events).

No sponsor's credit is acceptable which, in the Authority's opinion, would publicize directly or indirectly any goods or services so excluded.

A sponsor is not acceptable for a particular programme if his advertisements could not (under the Advertising Code) appear in or around that programme.

(ii) Political Sponsorship

Any organization whose aims and objectives are wholly or mainly of a political nature is prohibited from cable programme sponsorship.

Sponsorship by non-political organizations is not acceptable where the sponsoring of a programme is directed towards any political end or has any relation to any industrial dispute.

(iii) News and Current Affairs

News and current affairs programmes may not be sponsored other than with the specific approval of the Authority.

Notes for guidance

(The numbered paragraphs correspond to the sections of the Code.)

2. The arrangements described in Section 2 will not be treated as applying where the programmer has been influential in setting up the event and/or the sponsorship of it. In this situation the rules about prohibited sponsors (see Section 6) will apply and, in particular, sponsorship of an event by a cigarette brand or tobacco house will not be acceptable. Where the event takes place in the UK, the programmer's influence will normally be presumed. This would not prevent programmers from purchasing the rights to overseas tobacco sponsored events based on the material's programming merits.

4. (i) Underwriting

Suitable expressions might include 'presented by' or 'brought to you by'.

4. (ii) Commissioning

Each programmer is encouraged to develop uniform presentation of credits where programmes have been

commissioned. Devices to achieve this might i
standardizing the typeface, colour and text
announcement so that it becomes readily accept
label in much the same way as 'There now follows a Party
Political Broadcast . . .'

6. (i) The use of a tobacco company's house name as an
underwriting or commissioning credit would normally
be considered unacceptable by the Authority as indirectly
publicizing cigarettes.

6. (ii) Political Sponsorship

This clause places no restrictions on cable operators'
ability to offer local channel access to both political and
non-political organizations representing a wide diversity
of opinion, nor on the freedom of programmers to offer
'opinion' time to anyone they wish, subject only to the
Programme Code.

The sponsorship of political programming is not ruled
out. The test for considering sponsorship by a non-
political organization or company should be whether the
decision to sponsor that programme has the purpose of
prompting a political end or is related to an industrial
dispute. In making this judgement, the interest of the
sponsor in the political end or the industrial dispute will
clearly be relevant.

6. (iv) News

This clause places no restriction on documentary
sponsorship. Programmers should consult the Authority
in advance if in doubt about the distinction between
News and Current Affairs and documentary material.

The Authority has a particular duty to ensure the
impartiality of news and therefore will consider
sponsorship in this area only by underwriting.

'brief'

The Authority would not normally expect copylines contained in
credits given under Section 3 to exceed five seconds.

'short'

The Authority would not normally expect copylines contained in
credits given under Section 4 to exceed ten seconds.

'undue emphasis'

Some considerations might be

(i) Are these products/services consonant with the argument

or germane to the plot of the programme, or are they obtrusive and contrived? Would a viewer be left wondering why they had been included?

(ii) Is the camera dwelling on the products/services? Are they in close-up for no good reason?

(iii) Without the opening or closing credits, would it be possible to deduce the identity of the sponsor?

Quoted with permission.

Appendix 3 **Addresses**

Arts Council of Great Britain
105 Piccadilly
London W1V 0AU
01–629 9495

Regional Arts Associations (RAAs)
Council of Regional Arts Associations (CORAA)
Litton Lodge
13A Clifton Road
Winchester
Hampshire SO22 5BP
0962 51063
This is the secretariat for the RAAs and exists for the coordi-
nation of their work and to promote their interests at a national
level.

Buckinghamshire Arts Association
55 High Street
Aylesbury
Bucks HP20 1SA
0296 34704

Eastern Arts
8–9 Bridge Street
Cambridge CB2 1UA
0223 357596
Bedfordshire, Cambridgeshire, Essex, Hertfordshire, Norfolk,
Suffolk

East Midlands Arts
Mountfields House
Forest Road
Loughborough
Leicestershire LE11 3HU
0509 218292

Derbyshire (excluding High Peak district), Leicestershire, Northamptonshire, Nottinghamshire

Greater London Arts
25–31 Tavistock Place
London WC1H 9SF
01–388 2211
The area of the 32 London boroughs and the City of London

Lincolnshire and Humberside Arts
St Hugh's
Newport
Lincoln LN1 3DN
0522 33555

Merseyside Arts
Bluecoat Chambers
School Lane
Liverpool L1 3BX
051–709 0671
Metropolitan County of Merseyside, district of West Lancashire, Ellesmere Port and Halton districts of Cheshire

Northern Arts
10 Osborne Terrace
Newcastle upon Tyne NE2 1NZ
0632 816334
Cleveland, Cumbria, Durham, Northumberland, Metropolitan County of Tyne and Wear

North West Arts
12 Harter Street
Manchester M1 6HY
061–228 3062
Greater Manchester, High Peak district of Derbyshire, Lancashire (except district of West Lancashire), Cheshire (except Ellesmere Port and Halton districts)

South East Arts
9–10 Crescent Road
Tunbridge Wells
Kent TN1 2LU
0892 41666
Kent, Surrey, East Sussex

Southern Arts
19 Southgate Street
Winchester
Hampshire SO23 9DQ
0962 55099
Berkshire, Hampshire, Isle of Wight, Oxfordshire, West Sussex, Wiltshire, districts of Bournemouth, Christchurch and Poole

South West Arts
Bradninch Place
Gandy Street
Exeter EX4 3LS
0392 218188
Avon, Cornwall, Devon, Dorset (except districts of Bournemouth, Christchurch and Poole), Gloucestershire, Somerset

West Midlands Arts
Brunswick Terrace
Stafford ST16 1BZ
0785 59231
County of Hereford and Worcester, Metropolitan County of West Midlands, Shropshire, Staffordshire, Warwickshire

Yorkshire Arts Association
Glyde House
Glydegate
Bradford
Yorkshire BD5 0BQ
0274 723051

Arts Council of Northern Ireland
181a Stranmillis Road
Belfast BT9 5DU
0232 663591

Association for Business Sponsorship of the Arts
2 Chester Street
London SW1X 7BB
01–235 9781

Association for Business Sponsorship of the Arts
Room 613, Scottish Post Office Board
Post Office Headquarters Scotland
West Port House
102 West Port
Edinburgh EH3 9HS
031–228 7346

Business Committee for the Arts Inc
1775 Broadway
New York, NY 10019
USA
212–664 0600

Cable Authority
Gillingham House,
38 Gillingham Street
London SW1V 1HU
01–821 6161

Central Council of Physical Recreation
Francis House
Francis Street
London SW1P 1DE
01–828 3163

Charity Commission
14 Ryder Place
London SW1Y 6AH
01–214 6000

The English Tourist Board
Thames Tower
Black's Road
London W6 9EL
01–846 9000

Essex County Council
Planning Department
Globe House
New Street
Chelmsford
Essex CM1 1LF
0245 352232

Independent Broadcasting Authority
70 Brompton Road
London SW3 1EY
01–584 7011

The Institute of Sports Sponsorship
Francis House
Francis Street
London SW1P 1DE
01–828 8771

The Royal Society for the Protection of Birds
The Lodge
Sandy
Bedfordshire SG19 2DL
0767 80551

Scottish Arts Council
19 Charlotte Square
Edinburgh EH2 4DF
031–226 6051

The Scottish Sports Council
1 St Colme Street
Edinburgh EH3 6AA
031–225 8411

The Sponsorship Association
32 Sekforde Street
Clerkenwell Green
London EC1R 0HH
01–251 2505

Sponsorship News
PO Box 66
Wokingham
Berkshire RG11 4RQ
0734 730770

Sports Aid Foundation
16 Upper Woburn Place
London WC1H 0QN
01–387 9380

Sportscan
Baltic Centre
Great West Road
Brentford
Middx TW8 9S0

The Sports Council
16 Upper Woburn Place
London WC1H 0QN
01–388 1277
(The Sports Sponsorship Advisory Service is also at this
address.)

Regional Offices of the Sports Council
Eastern Region
26–28 Bromham Road
Bedford MK40 2QD
0234 45222

East Midland Region
Grove House
Bridgford Road
West Bridgford
Nottingham NG2 6AP
0602 821887

Greater London and South East Region
PO Box 480
Crystal Palace National Sports Centre
Ledrington Road
London SE19 2BQ
01–778 8600

Northern Region
County Court Building
Hallgarth Street
Durham DH1 3PB
0385 49595

North West Region
Byrom House
Quay Street
Manchester M3 5FJ
061–834 0338

Southern Region
51a Church Street
Caversham
Reading
Berkshire
0734 483311

South West Region
Ashlands House
Ashlands
Crewkerne
Somerset TA18 7LQ
0460 73491

West Midlands Region
Metropolitan House
1 Hagley Road
Five Ways
Birmingham B16 8TT
021–454 3808

Yorkshire and Humberside Region
Coronet House
Queen Street
Leeds LS1 4PW
0532 436443

The Sports Council for Northern Ireland
The House of Sport
2a Upper Malone Road
Belfast BT9 5LA
0232 661222

The Sports Council for Wales
Sophia Gardens
Cardiff CF1 9SW
0222 397571

Welsh Arts Council
9 Museum Place
Cardiff CF1 3NX
0222 394711

World Wildlife Fund – UK
Corporate Fund Raising Department
Panda House
11–13 Ockford Road
Godalming
Surrey GU7 1QU
04868 20551

Index